THE WORKS OF
EUGENE FIELD

Vol. I

THE WRITINGS IN PROSE AND VERSE OF EUGENE FIELD

A LITTLE BOOK OF WESTERN VERSE ❧ ❧ ❧ ❧

CHARLES SCRIBNER'S SONS ❧ NEW YORK ❧ 1900

TO

MARY FIELD FRENCH

A dying mother gave to you
   Her child a many years ago ;
How in your gracious love he grew,
   You know, dear, patient heart, you know.

The mother's child you fostered then
   Salutes you now and bids you take
These little children of his pen
   And love them for the author's sake.

To you I dedicate this book,
   And, as you read it line by line,
Upon its faults as kindly look
   As you have always looked on mine.

Tardy the offering is and weak ; —
   Yet were I happy if I knew
These children had the power to speak
   My love and gratitude to you.

             E. F.

Go, little book, and if an one would speak thee ill, let him bethink him that thou art the child of one who loves thee well. ❦ ❦

EUGENE FIELD

A MEMORY

WHEN those we love have passed away; when from our lives something has gone out; when with each successive day we miss the presence that has become a part of ourselves, and struggle against the realization that it is with us no more, we begin to live in the past and thank God for the gracious boon of memory. Few of us there are who, having advanced to middle life, have not come to look back on the travelled road of human existence in thought of those who journeyed awhile with us, a part of all our hopes and joyousness, the sharers of all our ambitions and our pleasures, whose mission has been fulfilled and who have left us with the mile-stones of years still seeming to stretch out on the path ahead. It is then that memory comes with its soothing influence, telling us of the happiness that was ours and comforting us with the ever recurring thought of the pleasures of that travelled road. For it is happiness to walk and talk with a brother for forty years, and it is happiness to know that the surety of that brother's affection, the knowledge of the greatness of his heart and the nobility of his mind, are not for one memory alone but may be publicly attested for admiration and emulation. That it has fallen to me to speak to the world of my brother as I knew him I rejoice. I do not fear that, speaking as a brother, I shall crowd the laurel wreaths upon him, for to this extent he lies in peace already honored; but if I can show him to the world, not as a poet but as a man,—if I may lead men to see more of that goodness, sweetness, and gentleness that were in him, I shall the more bless the memory that has survived.

My brother was born in St. Louis in 1850. Whether the exact day was September 2 or September 3 was a question over which he was given to speculation, more particularly in later years, when he was accustomed to discuss it frequently and with much earnestness. In his youth the anniversary was generally held to be September 2, perhaps the result of a half-humorous remark by my father that Oliver Cromwell had died September 3, and he could not reconcile this date to the thought that it was an important anniversary to one of his children. Many years after, when my uncle, Charles Kellogg Field, of Vermont, published the genealogy of the Field family, the original date, September 3, was restored, and from that time my brother accepted it, although with each recurring anniversary the controversy was gravely renewed, much to the amusement of the family and always to his own perplexity. In November, 1856, my mother died, and, at the breaking up of the family in St. Louis, my brother and myself, the last of six children, were taken to Amherst, Massachusetts, by our cousin, Miss Mary F. French, who took upon herself the care and responsibility of our bringing up. How nobly and self-sacrificingly she entered upon and discharged those duties my brother gladly testified in the beautiful dedication of his first published poems, "A Little Book of

Western Verse," wherein he honored the
"gracious love" in which he grew, and
bade her look as kindly on the faults of his
pen as she had always looked on his own.
For a few years my brother attended a private school for boys in Amherst ; then, at
the age of fourteen, he was intrusted to the
care of Rev. James Tufts, of Monson, one of
those noble instructors of the blessed old
school who are passing away from the arena
of education in America. By Mr. Tufts he
was fitted for college, and from the enthu-
siasm of this old scholar he caught perhaps
the inspiration for the love of the classics
which he carried through life. In the fall
of 1868 he entered Williams College — the
choice was largely accidental — and remained
there one year. My father died in the summer of 1869, and my brother chose as his
guardian Professor John William Burgess,
now of Columbia University, New York
City. When Professor Burgess, later in the
summer, accepted a call to Knox College,
Galesburg, Illinois, my brother accompanied
him and entered that institution, but the
restlessness which was so characteristic of

him in youth asserted itself after another year and he joined me, then in my junior year at the University of Missouri, at Columbia. It was at this institution that he finished his education so far as it related to prescribed study.

Shortly after attaining his majority he went to Europe, remaining six months in France and Italy. From this European trip have sprung the absurd stories which have represented him as squandering thousands of dollars in the pursuit of pleasure. Unquestionably he had the not unnatural extravagance which accompanies youth and a most generous disposition, for he was lavish and open-handed all through life to an unusual degree, but at no time was he particularly given to wild excesses, and the fact that my father's estate, which was largely realty, had shrunk perceptibly during the panic days of 1873 was enough to make him soon reach the limit of even moderate extravagance. At the same time many good stories have been told illustrative of his contempt for money, and it is eminently characteristic of his lack of the Puritan regard for small things that one day he approached my father's executor, Hon. M. L. Gray, of St. Louis, with a request for seventy-five dollars.

"But," objected this cautious and excellent man, "I gave you seventy-five dollars only yesterday, Eugene. What did you do with that?"

"Oh," replied my brother, with an impatient and scornful toss of the head, "I believe I bought some postage stamps."

Before going to Europe he had met Miss Julia Sutherland Comstock, of St. Joseph, Missouri, the sister of a college friend, and the attachment which was formed led to their marriage in October, 1873. Much of his tenderest and sweetest verse was inspired by love for the woman who became his wife, and the dedication to the "Second Book of Verse" is hardly surpassed for depth of affection and daintiness of sentiment, while "Lover's Lane, St. Jo.," is the very essence of loyalty, love, and reminiscential ardor. At the time of his marriage my brother realized the importance of going to work in earnest, and shortly before the appointment of the wedding-day he entered upon the active duties of journalism, which he never relinquished during life. These duties, with the exception of the year he passed in Europe with his family in 1889-90, were confined to the West. He began as a paragrapher in St. Louis, quickly achieving somewhat more than a merely local reputation. For a time he was in St. Joseph, and for eighteen months following January 1880 he lived in Kansas City, removing thence to Denver. In 1883 he came to Chicago at the solicitation of Melville E. Stone, then editor of the Chicago Daily News, retaining his connection with the News and its offspring, the Record, until his death. Thus hastily have been skimmed over the bare outlines of his life.

The formative period of my brother's youth was passed in New England, and to the influences which still prevail in and around her peaceful hills and gentle streams, the influences of a sturdy stock which has sent so many good and brave men to the West for the upbuilding of the country and the upholding of what is best in Puritan tradition, he gladly acknowledged he owed much that was strong and enduring. While he gloried

in the West and remained loyal to the section
which gave him birth, and in which he chose
to cast his lot, he was not the less proud of
his New England blood and not the less conscious of the benefits of a New England
training. His boyhood was similar to that
of other boys brought up with the best surroundings in a Massachusetts village, where
the college atmosphere prevailed. He had
his boyish pleasures and his trials, his share
of that queer mixture of nineteenth-century
worldliness and almost austere Puritanism
which is yet characteristic of many New
England families. The Sabbath was a veritable day of judgment, and in later years he
spoke humorously of the terrors of those all-
day sessions in church and Sunday-school,
though he never failed to acknowledge the
benefits he had derived from an enforced
study of the Bible. "If I could be grateful
to New England for nothing else," he would
say, "I should bless her forevermore for
pounding me with the Bible and the spelling-
book." And in proof of the earnestness of
this declaration he spent many hours in Bos-
ton a year or two ago, trying to find "one

of those spellers that temporarily made me lose my faith in the system of the universe."

It is easy at this day to look back three decades and note the characteristics which appeared trivial enough then, but which, clinging to him and developing, had a marked effect on his manhood and on the direction of his talents. As a boy his fondness for pets amounted to a passion, but unlike other boys he seemed to carry his pets into a higher sphere and to give them personality. For each pet, whether dog, cat, bird, goat, or squirrel—he had the family distrust of a horse—he not only had a name, but it was his delight to fancy that each possessed a peculiar dialect of human speech, and each he addressed in the humorous manner conceived. He ignored the names in common use for domestic animals and chose or invented those more pleasing to his exuberant fancy. This conceit was always with him, and years afterward, when his children took the place of his boyish pets, he gratified his whim for strange names by ignoring those designated at the baptismal font and substituting freakish titles of his own riotous fancy. Indeed it must have been a tax on his imaginative powers. When in childhood he was conducting a poultry annex to the homestead, each chicken was properly instructed to respond to a peculiar call, and Finnikin, Minnikin, Winnikin, Dump, Poog, Boog, seemed to recognize immediately the queer intonations of their master with an intelligence that is not usually accorded to chickens. With this love for animal life was developed also that tenderness of heart which was so manifest in my brother's daily actions. One day—he was then a good-sized boy— he came into the house, and throwing himself on the sofa, sobbed for half an hour. One of the chickens hatched the day before had been crushed under his foot as he was walking in the chicken-house, and no murderer could have felt more keenly the pangs of remorse. The other boys looked on curiously at this exhibition of feeling, and it was indeed an unusual outburst. But it was strongly characteristic of him through life, and nothing would so excite his anger as cruelty to an animal, while every neglected, friendless dog or persecuted cat always found in him a champion and a friend.

In illustration of this humane instinct it is recalled that a few weeks before he died a lady visiting the house found his room swarming with flies. In response to her exclamation of astonishment he explained that a day or two before he had seen a poor, half-frozen fly on the window-pane outside, and he had been moved by a kindly impulse to open the window and admit her. "And this," he added, "is what I get for it. That ungrateful creature is, as you perceive, the grandmother of eight thousand nine hundred and seventy-six flies!"

That the birds that flew about his house in Buena Park knew his voice has been demonstrated more than once. He would keep bread crumbs scattered along the window-sill for the benefit, as he explained, of the blue jays and the robins who were not in their usual robust health or were too overcome by the heat to make customary exertion. If the jays were particularly noisy he would go into the yard and expostulate with them in a tone of friendly reproach, whereupon, the family affirms, they would apparently apologize and fly away. Once he maintained at considerable expense a thoroughly hopeless and useless donkey, and it was his custom, when returning from the office at any hour of the night, to go into the back yard and say " Poor old Don " in a bass voice that carried a block away, whereupon old Don would lift up his own voice with a melancholy bray of welcome that would shake the windows and start the neighbors from their slumbers. Old Don is passing his declining years in an " Old Kentucky home," and the robins and the blue jays as they return with the spring will look in vain for the friend who fed them at the window.

The family dog at Amherst, which was immortalized many years later with " The Bench-Legged Fyce," and which was known in his day to hundreds of students at the college on account of his surpassing lack of beauty, rejoiced originally in the honest name of Fido, but my brother rejected this name as commonplace and unworthy, and straightway named him " Dooley " on the presumption that there was something Hibernian in his face. It was to Dooley that he wrote his first poem, a parody on "O Had I Wings Like a Dove," a song then in great vogue. Near the head of the village street was the home of the Emersons, a large frame house, now standing for more than a century, and in the great yard in front stood the magnificent elms which are the glory of the Connecticut valley. Many times the boys, returning from school, would linger to cool off in the shade of these glorious trees, and it was on one of these occasions that my brother put into the mouth of Dooley his maiden effort in verse:

> O had I wings like a dove I would fly,
>   Away from this world of fleas;
> I'd fly all round Miss Emerson's yard,
>   And light on Miss Emerson's trees.

Even this startling parody, which was regarded by the boys as a veritable stroke of genius, failed to impress the adult villagers with the conviction that a poet was budding. Yet how much of quiet humor and lively imagination is betrayed by these four lines.   How easy it is now to look back at the small boy and picture him sympathizing with his little friend tormented by the heat and the pests of his kind, and making him sigh for the rest that seemed to lurk in the rustling leaves of the stately elms.   Perhaps it was not astonishing poetry even for a child, but was there not something in the fancy, the sentiment, and the rhythm which bespoke far more than ordinary appreciation? Is it not this same quality of alert and instinctive sympathy which has run through Eugene Field's writings and touched the spring of popular affection?

Dooley went to the dog heaven many years ago.   Finnikin and Poog and Boog and the scores of boyhood friends that followed them have passed to their Pythagorean reward; but the boy who first found in them the delight of companionship and the kindlings of imagination retained all the youthful impulses which made him for nearly half a century the lover of animal life and the gentle singer of the faithful and the good.

Comradeship was the indispensable factor in my brother's life.   It was strong in his youth; it grew to be an imperative necessity in later years. In the theory that it is sometimes good to be alone he had little or no faith. Even when he was at work in his study, when it was almost essential to thought that he should be undisturbed, he was never quite content unless aware of the presence of human beings near at hand, as betrayed by their voices. It is customary to think of a poet wandering off in the great solitudes, standing alone in contemplation of the wonderful work of nature, on the cliffs overlooking the ocean, in the paths of the forest or on the mountain side. My brother was not of this order. That he was primarily and essentially a poet of humanity and not of nature does not argue that he was insensible to natural beauty or natural grandeur. Nobody could have been more keenly susceptible to the influences of nature in their temperamental effect, and perhaps this may explain that he did not love nature the less but that he prized companionship more. If nature pleased him he longed for a friend to share his pleasure; if it appalled him he turned from it with repugnance and fear.

Throughout his writings may be found the most earnest appreciation of the joyousness and loveliness of a beautiful landscape, but as he would share it intellectually with his readers so it was a necessity that he could not seek it alone as an actuality. In his boyhood, in the full glory of a perfect day, he loved to ramble through the woods and meadows, and delighted in the azure tints of the far-away Berkshire hills; and later in life he was keen to notice and admire the soft harmonies of landscape, but with a change in weather or with the approach of a storm the poet would be lost in the timidity and distrust of a child.

Companionship with him meant cheerfulness. His horror of gloom and darkness was almost morbid. From the tragedies of life he instinctively shrank, and large as was his sympathy, and generous and genuine his affection, he was often prompted to run from suffering and to betray what must have been a constitutional terror of distress. He did not hesitate to acknowledge this characteristic, and sought to atone for it by writing the most tender and touching lines to those to whom he believed he owed a gift of comfort and strength. His private letters to friends in adversity or bereavement were beautiful in their simplicity and honest and outspoken love, for he was not ashamed to let his friends see how much he thought of them. And even if the emotional quality, which asserts itself in the nervous and artistic temperament, made him realize that he could not trust himself, that same quality gave him a personality marvelous in its magnetism. Both as boy and man he made friends everywhere, and that he retained them to the last speaks for the whole-heartedness and genuineness of his nature.

To two weaknesses he frankly confessed: that he was inclined to be superstitious and that he was afraid of the dark. One of these he stoutly defended, asserting that he who was not fearful in the dark was a dull clod, utterly devoid of imagination. From his earliest childhood my brother was a devourer of fairy tales, and he continually stored his mind with fantastic legends, which found a vent in new shapes in his verses and prose tales. In the ceiling of one of his dens a trap-door led into the attic, and as this door was open he seriously contemplated closing it, because, as he said, he fancied that queer things would come down in the night and spirit him away. It is not to be inferred that he thus remained in a condition of actual fear, but it is true that he was imaginative to the degree of acute nervousness, and, like a child, associated light with safety and darkness with the uncanny and the supernatural. It was after all the better for his songs that it was so, else they might not have been filled with that cheery optimism which praised the happiness of sunlight and warmth, and sought to lift humanity from the darkness of despondency.

This weakness, or intellectual virtue as he pleasantly regarded it, was perhaps rather stronger in him as a man than in his boyhood. He has himself declared that he wrote "Seein' Things at Night" more to solace his own feelings than to delineate the sufferings of childhood, however aptly it may describe them. And when he put into rhythm that "any color, so long as it 's red, is the color that suits me best," he spoke not only as a poet but as a man, for red conveyed to him the idea of warmth and cheeriness, and seemed to express to him in color his temperamental demand. All through his life he pandered to these feelings instead of seeking to repress them, for to this extent there was little of the Puritan in his nature, and as he believed that happiness comes largely from within, so he felt that it is not un-Christian philosophy to avoid as far as possible whatever may cloud and render less acceptable one's own existence.

The literary talent of my brother is not easily traceable to either branch of the family. In fact it was tacitly accepted that he would be a lawyer as his father and grandfather had been before him, but the futility of this arrangement was soon manifest, and surely no man less temperamentally equipped for the law ever lived. It has been said of the Fields, speaking generally of the New England division, that they were well adapted to be either musicians or actors, though the talent for music or mimicry has been in no case carried out of private life save in my brother's public readings. Eugene had more than a boy's share of musical talent, but he never cultivated it, preferring to use the fine voice with which he was endowed for recitation, of which he was always fond. Acting was his strongest boyish passion. Even as a child he was a wonderful mimic and thereby the delight of his playmates and the terror of his teachers. He organized a stock company among the small boys of the village and gave performances in the barn of one of the less scrupulous neighbors, but whether for pins or pennies memory does not suggest. He assigned the parts and always reserved for himself the eccentric character and the low comedy, caring nothing for the heroic or the sentimental. One of the plays performed was Lester Wallack's "Rosedale" with Eugene in the dual role of the low comedian and the heavy villain. At this time also he delighted in monologues, imitations of eccentric types, or what Mr. Sol. Smith Russell calls "comics," a word which always amused Eugene and which he frequently used. This fondness for parlor readings and private theatricals he carried through college, remaining steadfast to the "comics" until a few years ago, when he began to give public readings, and discovered that he was capable of higher and more effective work. It was in fact his versatility that made him the most accomplished and the most popular author-entertainer in America. Before he went into journalism the more sedate of his family connections were in constant fear lest he should adopt the profession of the actor, and he held it over them as a good-natured threat. On one occasion, failing to get a coveted appropriation from the executor of the estate, he said calmly to the worthy man: "Very well. I must have money for my living expenses. If you cannot advance it to me out of the estate I shall be compelled to go on the stage. But as I cannot keep my own name I have decided to assume yours, and shall have lithographs struck off at once. They will read, 'To-night, M. L. Gray, Banjo and Specialty Artist.'" The appropriation was immediately forthcoming.

It is in no sense depreciatory of my brother's attainments in life to say that he gave no evidence of precocity in his studies in childhood. On the contrary he was somewhat slow in development, though this was due not so much to a lack of natural ability — he learned easily and quickly when so disposed — as to a fondness for the hundred diversions which occupy a wide-awake boy's time. He possessed a marked talent for caricature, and not a small part of the study hours was devoted to amusing pictures of his teachers, his playmates, and his pets. This habit of drawing, which was wholly without instruction, he always preserved, and it was his honest opinion, even at the height of his success in authorship, that he would have been much greater as a caricaturist than as a writer. Until he was thirty years of age he wrote a fair-sized legible hand, but about that time he adopted the microscopic penmanship which has been so widely reproduced, using for the purpose very fine-pointed pens. With his manuscript he took the greatest pains, often going to infinite trouble to illuminate his letters. Among his friends these letters are held as curiosities of literature, hardly more for the quaint sentiments expressed than for the queer designs

in colored inks which embellished them.
He was specially fond of drawing weird
elves and gnomes, and would spend an hour
or two decorating with these comical figures
a letter he had written in ten minutes. He
was as fastidious with the manuscript for
the office as if it had been a specimen copy
for exhibition, and it was always understood
that his manuscript should be returned to
him after it had passed through the printers'
hands. In this way all the original copies
of his stories and poems have been preserved,
and those which he did not give to friends
as souvenirs have been bound for his children.

A taste for literary composition might not
have passed, as doubtless it did pass, so
many years unnoticed, had he been deficient
in other talents, and had he devoted himself exclusively to writing. But as a boy he
was fond, though in a less degree than many
boys, of athletic sports, and his youthful de-
sire for theatrical entertainments, pen carica-
turing, and dallying with his pets took up
much of his time. Yet he often gave way
to a fondness for composition, and there is

in the family possession a sermon which he wrote before he was ten years of age, in which he showed the results of those arduous Sabbath days in the old Congregational meeting-house. And at one time, when yet very young, he was at the head of a flourishing boys' paper, while at another, fresh from the inspiration of a blood-curdling romance in a New York Weekly, he prepared a series of tales of adventure which, unhappily, have not been preserved. In his college days he was one of the associate editors of the university magazine, and while at that time he had no serious thought of devoting his life to literature, his talents in that direction were freely confessed. From my father, whose studious habits in life had made him not only eminent at the bar but profoundly conversant with general literature, he had inherited a taste for reading, and it was this omnivorous passion for books that led my brother to say that his education had only begun when he fancied that it had left off. In boyhood he contracted that fascinating but highly injurious habit of reading in bed, which he subsequently extolled with great fervor; and as he grew older the habit increased upon him until he was obliged to admit that he could not enjoy literature unless he took it horizontally. If a friend expostulated with him, advising him to give up tobacco, reading in bed, and late hours, he said: "And what have we left in life if we give up all our bad habits?"

That the poetic instinct was always strong within him there has never been room to question, but, perhaps, for the reasons before assigned, it was tardy in making its way outward. For years his mind lay fallow and receptive, awaiting the occasion which should develop the true inspiration of the poet. He was accustomed to speak of himself, and too modestly, as merely a versifier, but his own experience should have contradicted this estimate, for his first efforts at verse were singularly halting in mechanical construction, and he was well past his twenty-fifth year before he gave to the world any verse worthy the name. What might be called the "curse of comedy" was on him, and it was not until he threw off that yoke and gave expression to the better and the sweeter thoughts within him that, as with Bion, "the voice of song flowed freely from the heart." It seems strange that a man who became a master of the art of mechanism in verse should have been deficient in this particular at a period comparatively late, but it merely illustrates the theory of gradual development and marks the phases of life through which, with his character of many sides, he was compelled to pass. He was nearly thirty when he wrote "Christmas Treasures," the first poem he deemed worthy, and very properly, of preservation, and the publication of this tender commemoration of the death of a child opened the springs of sentiment and love for childhood destined never to run dry while life endured.

In journalism he became immediately successful, not so much for adaptability to the treadmill of that calling as for the brightness and distinctive character of his writing. He easily established a reputation as a humorist, and while he fairly deserved the title he often regretted that he could not entirely shake it off. His powers of perception were phe-

nomenally keen, and he detected the peculiarities of people with whom he was thrown
in contact almost at a glance, while his gift
of mimicry was such that after a minute's
interview he could burlesque the victim to
the life, even emphasizing the small details
which had been apparently too minute to attract the special notice of those who were
acquaintances of years' standing.   This fac-
ulty he carried into his writing, and it proved
immensely valuable, for, with his quick appreciation of the ludicrous and his power of
delineating personal peculiarities his sketches
were remarkable for their resemblances even
when he was indulging apparently in the
wildest flights of imagination.   It is to be
regretted that much of his newspaper work,
covering a period of twenty years, was ne-
cessarily so full of purely local color that its
brilliancy could not be generally appreciated.
For it is as if an artist had painted a wondrous picture, clever enough in the general
view, but full of a significance hidden to the
world.

Equally facile was he in the way of adap-
tation.   He could write a hoax worthy of

Poe, and one of his humors of imagination was sufficiently subtle and successful to excite comment in Europe and America, and to call for an explanation and denial from a distinguished Englishman. He lived in Denver only a few weeks when he was writing verse in miners' dialect which has been rightly placed at the head of that style of composition. No matter where he wandered, he speedily became imbued with the spirit of his surroundings, and his quickly and accurately gathered impressions found vent in his pen, whether he was in "St. Martin's Lane" in London, with "Mynheer Von Der Bloom" in Amsterdam, or on the "Schnellest Zug" from Hanover to Leipzig.

At the time of my brother's arrival in Chicago, in 1883—he was then in his thirty-fourth year—he had performed an immense amount of newspaper work, but had done little or nothing of permanent value or with any real literary significance. But despite the fact that he had lived up to that time in the smaller cities he had a large number of acquaintances and a certain following in the journalistic and artistic world, of which from the very moment of his entrance into journalism he never had been deprived. His immense fund of good humor, his powers as a story-teller, his admirable equipment as an entertainer, and the whole-hearted way with which he threw himself into life and the pleasures of living attracted men to him and kept him the centre of the multitude that prized his fascinating companionship. His fellows in journalism furthermore had been quick to recognize his talents, and no man was more widely "copied," as the technical expression goes. His early years in Chicago did not differ materially from those of the previous decade, but the enlarged scope gave greater play to his fancy and more opportunity for his talents as a master of satire. The publication of "The Denver Primer" and "Culture's Garland," while adding to his reputation as a humorist, happily did not satisfy him. He was now past the age of thirty-five, and a great psychical revolution was coming on. Though still on the sunny side of middle life, he was wearying of the cup of pleasure he had drunk so joyously, and was drawing away from the multitude and toward the companionship of those who loved books and bookish things, and who could sympathize with him in the aspirations for the better work, the consciousness of which had dawned. It was now that he began to apply himself diligently to the preparation for higher effort, and it is to the credit of journalism, which has so many sins to answer for, that in this he was encouraged beyond the usual fate of men who become slaves to that calling. And yet, though from this time he was privileged to be regarded one of the sweetest singers in American literature, and incomparably the noblest bard of childhood, though the grind of journalism was measurably taken from him, he chafed under the conviction that he was condemned to mingle the prosaic and the practical with the fanciful and the ideal, and that, having given hostages to fortune, he must conform even in a measure to the requirements of a position too lucrative to be cast aside. From this time also his physical condition, which never had been robust, began to show the effects of sedentary life, but the warning of a long siege of nervous dyspepsia was suffered to pass unheeded, and for five or six years he labored prodigiously, his mind expanding and his intellect growing more brilliant as the vital powers decayed.

It would seem that with the awakening of the consciousness of the better powers within him, with the realization that he was destined for a place in literature, my brother felt a quasi remorse for the years he fancied he had wasted. He was too severe with himself to understand that his comparative tardiness in arriving at the earnest, thoughtful stage of lifework was the inexorable law of gradual development which must govern the career of a man of his temperament, with his exuberant vitality and his showy talents. It was a serious mistake, but it was not the less a noble one. And now also the influences of home crept a little closer into his heart. His family life had not been without its tragedies of bereavement, and the death of his oldest boy in Germany had drawn him even nearer to the children who were growing up around him.

Much of his tenderest verse was inspired by affection for his family, and as some great shock is often essential to the revolution in a buoyant nature, so it seemed to require the oft-recurring tragedies of life to draw from him all that was noblest and sweetest in his sympathetic soul. Had the angel of death never hovered over the crib in my brother's home, had he never known the pangs and the heart-hunger which come when the little voice is stilled and the little chair is empty, he could not have written the lines which voice the great cry of humanity and the hope of reunion in immortality beyond the grave.

The flood of appeals for platform readings from cities and towns in all parts of the United States came too late for his physical strength and his ambition. Earlier in life he would have delighted in this form of travel and entertainment, but his nature had wonderfully changed, and, strong as were the financial inducements, he was loath to leave his family and circle of intimate friends, and the home he had just acquired. All of the time which he allotted for recreation he devoted to working around his grounds, in arranging and rearranging his large library, and in the disposition of his curios. For years he had been an indefatigable collector, and he took a boyish pleasure not only in his souvenirs of long journeys and distinguished men and women, but in the queer toys and trinkets of children which seemed to give him inspiration for much that was effective in childhood verse. To the careless observer the immense array of weird dolls and absurd toys in his working-room meant little more than an idiosyncratic passion for the anomalous, but those who were near to him knew what a connecting link they were between him and the little children of whom he wrote, and how each trumpet and drum, each "spinster doll," each little toy dog, each little tin soldier, played its part in the poems he sent out into the world. No writer ever made more persistent and consistent use of the material by which he was surrounded, or put a higher literary value on the little things which go to make up the sum of human existence.

Of the spiritual development of my brother

much might be said in conviction and in tenderness. He was not a man who discussed religion freely; he was associated with no religious denomination, and he professed no creed beyond the brotherhood of mankind and the infinitude of God's love and mercy. In childhood he had been reared in much of the austerity of the Puritan doctrine of the relation of this life to the hereafter, and much of the hardness and severity of Christianity, as still interpreted in many parts of New England, was forced upon him. As is not unusual in such cases, he rebelled against this conception of God and God's day, even while he confessed the intellectual advantages he had reaped from frequent compulsory communion with the Bible, and he many times declared that his children should not be brought up to regard religion and the Sabbath as a bugbear. What evolution was going on in his mind at the turning point in his life who can say? Who shall look into the silent soul of the poet and see the hope and confidence and joy that have come from out the chaos of strife and doubt? Yet who can read the verses, telling over and over the beautiful

story of Bethlehem, the glory of the Christ-
child and the comfort that comes from the
Teacher, and doubt that in those moments
he walked in the light of the love of God ?

It is true that no man living in a Christian
nation who is stirred by poetic instinct can
fail to recognize and pay homage to that
story of wonderful sweetness, the coming
of the Christ-child for the redemption of the
world. It is true that in commemoration
the poet may speak while the man within is
silent. But it is hardly true that he whose
generous soul responded to every principle
of Christ, the Teacher, pleading for humanity,
would sing over and over that tender song
of love and sacrifice as a mere poetic inspiration. As he slept my brother's soul was
called. Who shall say that it was not
summoned by that same angel song that
awakened "Little Boy Blue" ? Who shall
doubt that the smile of supreme peace and
rest which lingered on his face after that
noble spirit had departed spoke for the vic-
tory he had won, for the hope and belief
that had been justified, and for the happiness
he had gained ?

xliii

To have been with my brother in the last year of his life, to have seen the sweetening of a character already lovable to an unusual degree, to know now that in his unconscious preparation for the life beyond he was drawing closer to those he loved and who loved him, this is the tenderest memory, the most precious heritage. Not to have seen him in that year is never to realize the full beauty of his nature, the complete development of his nobler self, the perfect abandonment of all that might have been ungenerous and intemperate in one even less conscious of the weakness of mortality. He would say when chided for public expression of kind words to those not wholly deserving, that he had felt the sting of harshness and ungraciousness, and never again would he use his power to inflict suffering or wound the feelings of man or child. Who is there to wonder, then, that the love of all went out to him, and that the other triumphs of his life were as nothing in comparison with the grasp he maintained on popular affection? The day after his death a lady was purchasing flowers to send in sympathy for the mourning family, when she was approached by a poorly-clad little girl who timidly asked what she was going to do with so many roses. When she replied that she intended sending them to Mr. Field, the little one said that she wanted so much to send Mr. Field a rose, adding pathetically that she had no money. Deeply touched by the child's sorrowful earnestness the lady picked out a yellow rose and gave it to her, and when the coffin was lowered to the grave a wealth of wreaths and designs was strewn around to mark the spot, but down below the hand of the silent poet held only a little yellow rose, the tribute of a child who did not know him in life, but in whose heart nestled the love his songs had awakened and the magnetism of his great humanity had stirred.

A few hours after his spirit had gone a crippled boy came to the house and begged permission to go to the chamber. The wish was granted, and the boy hobbled to the bedside. Who he was, and in what manner my brother had befriended him, none of the family knew, but as he painfully picked his way down stairs the tears were streaming over his face, and the onlookers forgot their own sorrow in contemplation of his grief. The morning of the funeral, while the family stood around the coffin, the letter-carrier at Buena Park came into the room, and laying a bunch of letters at the foot of the bier said reverently: "There is your last mail, Mr. Field." Then turning with tears in his eyes, as if apologizing for an intrusion, he added: "He was always good to me and I loved him."

It was this affection of those in humbler life that seems to speak the more eloquently for the beneficence and the triumph of his life's work. No funeral could have been less ostentatious, yet none could have been more impressive in the multitude that overflowed the church, or more conformable to his tenacious belief in the democracy of man. People of eminence, of wealth, of fashion, were there, but they were swallowed up in the great congregation of those to whom we are bound by the ties of humanity and universal brotherhood, whose tears as they passed the bier of the dead singer were the earnest and the best tribute to him who sang for all. What greater blessing hath man than this? What stronger assurance can there be of happiness in that life where all is weighed in the scale of love, and where love is triumphant and eternal?

Sleep, my brother, in the perfect joy of an awakening to that happiness beyond the probationary life. Sleep in the assurance that those who loved you will always cherish the memory of that love as the tender inspiration of your gentle spirit. Sleep and dream that the songs you sang will still be sung when those who sing them now are sleeping with you. Sleep and take your rest as calmly and peacefully as you slept when your last "Good-Night" lengthened into eternity. And if the Horace you so merrily invoked comes to you in your slumber and bids you awake to that sweet cheer, that "fellowship that knows no end beyond the misty Stygian sea," tell him that the time has not yet come, and that there are those yet uncalled, to whom you have pledged the joyous meeting on yonder shore, and who would share with you the heaven your companionship would brighten.

ROSWELL MARTIN FIELD.

BUENA PARK, January, 1896.

xlvii

The Contents of this Little Book

CONTENTS

1

CONTENTS

✤

A Little Book of Western Verse.

✤

CASEY'S TABLE D'HÔTE

H, them days on Red Hoss Mountain, when the skies wuz fair
'nd blue,
When the money flowed like likker, 'nd the
folks wuz brave 'nd true!
When the nights wuz crisp 'nd balmy, 'nd
the camp wuz all astir,
With the joints all throwed wide open 'nd
no sheriff to demur!
Oh, them times on Red Hoss Mountain in
the Rockies fur away,—
There's no sich place nor times like them as
I kin find to-day!
What though the camp *hez* busted? I seem
to see it still
A-lyin', like it loved it, on that big 'nd warty
hill;

And I feel a sort of yearnin' 'nd a chokin' in
    my throat
When I think of Red Hoss Mountain 'nd of
    Casey's tabble dote!

Wal, yes; it 's true I struck it rich, but that
    don't cut a show
When one is old 'nd feeble 'nd it 's nigh his
    time to go;
The money that he 's got in bonds or carries
    to invest
Don't figger with a codger who has lived a
    life out West;
Us old chaps like to set around, away from
    folks 'nd noise,
'Nd think about the sights we seen and
    things we done when boys;
The which is why *I* love to set 'nd think of
    them old days
When all us Western fellers got the Colo-
    rado craze,—
And *that* is why I love to set around all day
    'nd gloat
On thoughts of Red Hoss Mountain 'nd of
    Casey's tabble dote.

This Casey wuz an Irishman,— you 'd know
    it by his name
And by the facial features appertainin' to the
    same.
He 'd lived in many places 'nd had done a
    thousand things,
From the noble art of actin' to the work of
    dealin' kings,
But, somehow, had n't caught on; so, drift-
    in' with the rest,
He drifted for a fortune to the undeveloped
    West,
And he come to Red Hoss Mountain when
    the little camp wuz new,
When the money flowed like likker, 'nd the
    folks wuz brave 'nd true;
And, havin' been a stewart on a Mississippi
    boat,
He opened up a caffy 'nd he run a tabble
    dote.

The bar wuz long 'nd rangy, with a mirrer
    on the shelf,
'Nd a pistol, so that Casey, when required,
    could help himself;

Down underneath there wuz a row of bottled
    beer 'nd wine,
'Nd a kag of Burbun whiskey of the run of
    '59;
Upon the walls wuz pictures of hosses 'nd
    of girls,—
Not much on dress, perhaps, but strong on
    records 'nd on curls!
The which had been identified with Casey
    in the past,—
The hosses 'nd the girls, I mean,— and both
    wuz mighty fast!
But all these fine attractions wuz of precious
    little note
By the side of what wuz offered at Casey's
    tabble dote.

There wuz half-a-dozen tables altogether in
    the place,
And the tax you had to pay upon your vittles
    wuz a case;
The boardin'-houses in the camp protested
    't wuz a shame
To patronize a robber, which this Casey wuz
    the same!

They said a case was robbery to tax for ary
    meal;
But Casey tended strictly to his biz, 'nd let
    'em squeal;
And presently the boardin'-houses all began
    to bust,
While Casey kept on sawin' wood 'nd layin'
    in the dust;
And oncet a trav'lin' editor from Denver City
    wrote
A piece back to his paper, puffin' Casey's
    tabble dote.

A tabble dote is different from orderin' aller
    cart:
In *one* case you git all there is, in *t' other,*
    only *part!*
And Casey's tabble dote began in French, —
    as all begin, —
And Casey's ended with the same, which is
    to say, with "vin;"
But in between wuz every kind of reptile,
    bird, 'nd beast,
The same like you can git in high-toned res-
    tauraws down east;

'Nd windin' up wuz cake or pie, with coffee
    demy tass,
Or, sometimes, floatin' Ireland in a soothin'
    kind of sass
That left a sort of pleasant ticklin' in a feller's
    throat,
'Nd made him hanker after more of Casey's
    tabble dote.

The very recollection of them puddin's 'nd
    them pies
Brings a yearnin' to my buzzum 'nd the
    water to my eyes;
'Nd seems like cookin' nowadays ain't what
    it used to be
In camp on Red Hoss Mountain in that year
    of '63;
But, maybe, it is better, 'nd, maybe, I'm to
    blame —
I'd like to be a-livin' in the mountains jest
    the same —
I'd like to live that life again when skies wuz
    fair 'nd blue,
When things wuz run wide open 'nd men
    wuz brave 'nd true;

III

Sir Tomas from his noblesse halle
   Did trend his path a somer's daye,
And to ye hoyden he did call
   And these ffull evill words did say:
"O wolde you weare a silken gown
   And binde your haire with ribands gay?
Then come with me to town!"

IV

But Madge, ye hoyden, shoke her head,—
   "I 'le be no lemman unto thee
For all your golde and gownes," shee said,
   "ffor Robin hath bespoken mee."
Then ben Sir Tomas sore despight,
   And back unto his hall went hee
With face as ashen white.

V

"O Robin, wilt thou wed this girl,
   Whenas she is so vaine a sprite?"
So spak ffull many an envious churle
   Unto that curteyse countrie wight.
But Robin did not pay no heede;
   And they ben wed a somer night
& danct upon ye meade.

VI

Then scarse ben past a yeare & daye
 Whan Robin toke unto his bed,
And long, long time therein he lay,
 Nor colde not work to earn his bread;
in soche an houre, whan times ben sore,
 Sr. Tomas came with haughtie tread
& knockit at ye doore.

VII

Saies: "Madge, ye hoyden, do you know
 how that you once despighted me?
But Ile forgiff an you will go
 my swete harte lady ffor to bee!"
But Madge, ye hoyden, heard noe more,—
 straightway upon her heele turnt shee,
& shote ye cottage doore.

VIII

Soe Madge, ye hoyden, did her parte
 whiles that ye years did come and go;
't was somer allwais in her harte,
 tho' winter strewed her head with snowe.
She toilt and span thro' all those years
 nor bid repine that it ben soe,
nor never shad noe teares.

IX

Whiles Robin lay within his bed,
  A divell came and whispered lowe,—
"Giff you will doe my will," he said,
  "None more of sickness you shall knowe!"
Ye which gave joy to Robin's soul—
  Saies Robin: "Divell, be it soe,
an that you make me whoale!"

X

That day, upp rising ffrom his bed,
  Quoth Robin: "I am well again!"
& backe he came as from ye dead,
  & he ben mickle blithe as when
he wooed his doxy long ago;
  & Madge did make ado & then
Her teares ffor joy did flowe.

XI

Then came that hell-born cloven thing—
  Saies: "Robin, I do claim your life,
and I hencefoorth shall be your king,
  and you shall do my evill strife.
Look round about and you shall see
  sr. Tomas' young and ffoolish wiffe—
a comely dame is shee!"

XII

Ye divell had him in his power,
  and not colde Robin say thereto:
Soe Robin from that very houre
  did what that divell bade him do;
He wooed and clipt, and on a daye
  sr. Tomas' wife and Robin flewe
a many leagues away.

XIII

Sir Tomas ben wood wroth and swore,
  And sometime strode thro' leaf & brake
and knockit at ye cottage door
  and thus to Madge, ye hoyden, spake:
Saies, "I wolde have you ffor mine own,
  So come with mee & bee my make,
syn tother birds ben flown."

XIV

But Madge, ye hoyden, bade him noe;
  Saies: "Robin is my swete harte still,
And, tho' he doth despight me soe,
  I mean to do him good for ill.
So goe, Sir Tomas, goe your way;
  ffor whiles I bee on live I will
ffor Robin's coming pray!"

XV

Soe Madge, ye hoyden, kneelt & prayed
   that Godde sholde send her Robin backe.
And tho' ye folke vast scoffing made,
   and tho' ye worlde ben colde and blacke,
And tho', as moneths dragged away,
   ye hoyden's harte ben like to crack
With griff, she still did praye.

XVI

Sicke of that divell's damnèd charmes,
   Aback did Robin come at last,
And Madge, ye hoyden, sprad her arms
   and gave a cry and held him fast;
And as she clong to him and cried,
   her patient harte with joy did brast,
& Madge, ye hoyden, died.

OLD ENGLISH LULLABY

HUSH, bonnie, dinna greit;
  Moder will rocke her sweete,—
    Balow, my boy!
When that his toile ben done,
Daddie will come anone,—
Hush thee, my lyttel one;
    Balow, my boy!

Gin thou dost sleepe, perchaunce
Fayries will come to daunce,—
    Balow, my boy!
Oft hath thy moder seene
Moonlight and mirkland queene
Daunce on thy slumbering een,—
    Balow, my boy!

Then droned a bomblebee
Saftly this songe to thee:
    " Balow, my boy!"

And a wee heather bell,
Pluckt from a fayry dell,
Chimed thee this rune hersell:
    "Balow, my boy!"

Soe, bonnie, dinna greit;
Moder doth rock her sweete,—
    Balow, my boy!
Give mee thy lyttel hand,
Moder will hold it and
Lead thee to balow land,—
    Balow, my boy!

THE BIBLIOMANIAC'S PRAYER

KEEP me, I pray, in wisdom's way
    That I may truths eternal seek;
I need protecting care to-day,—
    My purse is light, my flesh is weak.
So banish from my erring heart
    All baleful appetites and hints
Of Satan's fascinating art,
    Of first editions, and of prints.
Direct me in some godly walk
    Which leads away from bookish strife,
That I with pious deed and talk
    May extra-illustrate my life.

But if, O Lord, it pleaseth Thee
    To keep me in temptation's way,
I humbly ask that I may be
    Most notably beset to-day;

Let my temptation be a book,
    Which I shall purchase, hold, and keep,
Whereon when other men shall look,
    They 'll wail to know I got it cheap.
Oh, let it such a volume be
    As in rare copperplates abounds,
Large paper, clean, and fair to see,
    Uncut, unique, unknown to Lowndes.

THE LYTTEL BOY

SOMETIME there ben a lyttel boy
  That wolde not renne and play,
And helpless like that little tyke
  Ben allwais in the way.
"Goe, make you merrie with the rest,"
  His weary moder cried;
But with a frown he catcht her gown
  And hong untill her side.

That boy did love his moder well,
  Which spake him faire, I ween;
He loved to stand and hold her hand
  And ken her with his een;
His cosset bleated in the croft,
  His toys unheeded lay,—
He wolde not goe, but, tarrying soe,
  Ben allwais in the way.

Godde loveth children and doth gird
   His throne with soche as these,
And He doth smile in plaisaunce while
   They cluster at His knees;
And sometime, when He looked on earth
   And watched the bairns at play,
He kenned with joy a lyttel boy
   Ben allwais in the way.

And then a moder felt her heart
   How that it ben to-torne,—
She kissed eche day till she ben gray
   The shoon he used to worn;
No bairn let hold untill her gown,
   Nor played upon the floore,—
Godde's was the joy; a lyttel boy
   Ben in the way no more!

THE TRUTH ABOUT HORACE

IT is very aggravating
  To hear the solemn prating
Of the fossils who are stating
    That old Horace was a prude;
When we know that with the ladies
He was always raising Hades,
And with many an escapade his
    Best productions are imbued.

There 's really not much harm in a
Large number of his carmina,
But these people find alarm in a
    Few records of his acts;
So they 'd squelch the muse caloric,
And to students sophomoric
They 'd present as metaphoric
    What old Horace meant for facts.

We have always thought 'em lazy;
Now we adjudge 'em crazy!
Why, Horace was a daisy
That was very much alive!
And the wisest of us know him
As his Lydia verses show him,—
Go, read that virile poem,—
It is No. 25.

He was a very owl, sir,
And starting out to prowl, sir,
You bet he made Rome howl, sir,
Until he filled his date;
With a massic-laden ditty
And a classic maiden pretty
He painted up the city,
And Mæcenas paid the freight!

THE DEATH OF ROBIN HOOD

"GIVE me my bow," said Robin Hood,
   "An arrow give to me;
And where 't is shot mark thou that spot,
   For there my grave shall be."

Then Little John did make no sign,
   And not a word he spake;
But he smiled, altho' with mickle woe
   His heart was like to break.

He raised his master in his arms,
   And set him on his knee;
And Robin's eyes beheld the skies,
   The shaws, the greenwood tree.

The brook was babbling as of old,
   The birds sang full and clear,
And the wild-flowers gay like a carpet lay
   In the path of the timid deer.

"O Little John," said Robin Hood,
   "Meseemeth now to be
Standing with you so stanch and true
   Under the greenwood tree.

"And all around I hear the sound
   Of Sherwood long ago,
And my merry men come back again,—
   You know, sweet friend, you know!

"Now mark this arrow; where it falls,
   When I am dead dig deep,
And bury me there in the greenwood where
   I would forever sleep."

He twanged his bow.   Upon its course
   The clothyard arrow sped,
And when it fell in yonder dell,
   Brave Robin Hood was dead.

The sheriff sleeps in a marble vault,
   The king in a shroud of gold;
And upon the air with a chanted pray'r
   Mingles the mock of mould.

But the deer draw to the shady pool,
   The birds sing blithe and free,
And the wild-flow'rs bloom o'er a hidden
     tomb
   Under the greenwood tree.

"LOLLYBY, LOLLY, LOLLYBY"

LAST night, whiles that the curfew bell ben
   ringing,
I heard a moder to her dearie singing
      " Lollyby, lolly, lollyby."
And presently that chylde did cease hys
   weeping,
And on his moder's breast did fall a-sleeping,
      To "lolly, lolly, lollyby."

Faire ben the chylde unto his moder clinging,
But fairer yet the moder's gentle singing,—
      "Lollyby, lolly, lollyby."
And angels came and kisst the dearie smiling
In dreems while him hys moder ben beguil-
   ing
      With "lolly, lolly, lollyby!"

Then to my harte saies I, "Oh, that thy
    beating
Colde be assuaged by some swete voice re-
    peating
      'Lollyby, lolly, lollyby;'
That like this lyttel chylde I, too, ben sleeping
With plaisaunt phantasies about me creeping,
      To 'lolly, lolly, lollyby!'"

Sometime—mayhap when curfew bells are
    ringing—
A weary harte shall heare straunge voices
    singing,
      "Lollyby, lolly, lollyby;"
Sometime, mayhap, with Chrysts love round
    me streaming,
I shall be lulled into eternal dreeming
      With "lolly, lolly, lollyby."

HORACE AND LYDIA RECONCILED

HORACE

WHEN you were mine in auld lang
      syne,
And when none else your charms might
    ogle,
      I 'll not deny,
      Fair nymph, that I
Was happier than a Persian mogul.

LYDIA

Before *she* came — that rival flame! —
    (Was ever female creature sillier ?)
      In those good times,
      Bepraised in rhymes,
I was more famed than Mother Ilia!

HORACE

Chloe of Thrace! With what a grace
    Does she at song or harp employ her!

I 'd gladly die
If only I
Might live forever to enjoy her!

LYDIA

My Sybaris so noble is
    That, by the gods! I love him madly—
        That I might save
        Him from the grave
I 'd give my life, and give it gladly!

HORACE

What if ma belle from favor fell,
    And I made up my mind to shake her,
        Would Lydia, then,
        Come back again
And to her quondam flame betake her?

LYDIA

My other beau should surely go,
    And you alone should find me gracious;
        For no one slings
        Such odes and things
As does the lauriger Horatius!

OUR TWO OPINIONS

US two wuz boys when we fell out,—
    Nigh to the age uv my youngest now;
Don't rec'lect what 't wuz about,
    Some small deeff'rence, I 'll allow.
Lived next neighbors twenty years,
    A-hatin' each other, me 'nd Jim,—
He havin' *his* opinyin uv *me,*
    'Nd *I* havin' *my* opinyin uv *him.*

Grew up together 'nd would n't speak,
    Courted sisters, 'nd marr'd 'em, too;
'Tended same meetin'-house oncet a week,
    A-hatin' each other through 'nd through!
But when Abe Linkern asked the West
    F'r soldiers, we answered,— me 'nd Jim,—
He havin' *his* opinyin uv *me,*
    'Nd *I* havin' *my* opinyin uv *him.*

31

But down in Tennessee one night
   Ther' wuz sound uv firin' fur away,
'Nd the sergeant allowed ther' 'd be a fight
   With the Johnnie Rebs some time nex' day;
'Nd as I wuz thinkin' uv Lizzie 'nd home
   Jim stood afore me, long 'nd slim,—
He havin' *his* opinyin uv *me,*
   'Nd *I* havin' *my* opinyin uv *him.*

Seemed like we knew there wuz goin' to be
   Serious trouble f'r me 'nd him;
Us two shuck hands, did Jim 'nd me,
   But never a word from me or Jim!
He went *his* way 'nd *I* went *mine,*
   'Nd into the battle's roar went we,—
I havin' *my* opinyin uv Jim,
   'Nd *he* havin' *his* opinyin uv *me.*

Jim never come back from the war again,
   But I hain't forgot that last, last night
When, waitin' f'r orders, us two men
   Made up 'nd shuck hands, afore the fight.
'Nd, after it all, it 's soothin' to know
   That here *I* be 'nd yonder 's Jim,—
He havin' *his* opinyin uv *me,*
   'Nd *I* havin' *my* opinyin uv *him.*

MOTHER AND CHILD

ONE night a tiny dewdrop fell
   Into the bosom of a rose,—
"Dear little one, I love thee well,
   Be ever here thy sweet repose!"

Seeing the rose with love bedight,
   The envious sky frowned dark, and then
Sent forth a messenger of light
   And caught the dewdrop up again.

"Oh, give me back my heavenly child,—
   My love!" the rose in anguish cried;
Alas! the sky triumphant smiled,
   And so the flower, heart-broken, died.

ORKNEY LULLABY

A MOONBEAM floateth from the skies,
　　Whispering, "Heigho, my dearie!
I would spin a web before your eyes,—
A beautiful web of silver light,
Wherein is many a wondrous sight
Of a radiant garden leagues away,
Where the softly tinkling lilies sway,
And the snow-white lambkins are at play,—
　　Heigho, my dearie!"

A brownie stealeth from the vine
　　Singing, "Heigho, my dearie!
And will you hear this song of mine,—
A song of the land of murk and mist
Where bideth the bud the dew hath kist?
Then let the moonbeam's web of light
Be spun before thee silvery white,
And I shall sing the livelong night,—
　　Heigho, my dearie!"

34

The night wind speedeth from the sea,
     Murmuring, ''Heigho, my dearie!
I bring a mariner's prayer for thee;
So let the moonbeam veil thine eyes,
And the brownie sing thee lullabies;
But I shall rock thee to and fro,
Kissing the brow *he* loveth so,
And the prayer shall guard thy bed, I trow,—
     Heigho, my dearie!''

LITTLE MACK

THIS talk about the journalists that run
    the East is bosh,
We 've got a Western editor that 's little,
    but, O gosh!
He lives here in Mizzoora where the people
    are so set
In ante-bellum notions that they vote for
    Jackson yet;
But the paper he is running makes the rusty
    fossils swear,—
The smartest, likeliest paper that is printed
    anywhere!
And, best of all, the paragraphs are pointed
    as a tack,
        And that 's because they emanate
        From little Mack.

In architecture he is what you 'd call a chunky
    man,
As if he 'd been constructed on the summer
    cottage plan;
He has a nose like Bonaparte; and round his
    mobile mouth
Lies all the sensuous languor of the children
    of the South;
His dealings with reporters who affect a
    weekly bust
Have given to his violet eyes a shadow of
    distrust;
In glorious abandon his brown hair wanders
    back
        From the grand Websterian forehead
        Of little Mack.

No matter what the item is, if there 's an item
    in it,
You bet your life he 's on to it and nips it in
    a minute!
From multifarious nations, countries, mon-
    archies, and lands,
From Afric's sunny fountains and India's
    coral strands,

From Greenland's icy mountains and Si-
    loam's shady rills,
He gathers in his telegrams, and Houser
    pays the bills;
What though there be a dearth of news, he
    has a happy knack
        Of scraping up a lot of scoops,
            Does little Mack,

And learning?   Well he knows the folks of
    every tribe and age
That ever played a part upon this fleeting
    human stage;
His intellectual system 's so extensive and
    so greedy
That, when it comes to records, he 's a
    walkin' cyclopedy;
For having studied (and digested) all the
    books a-goin',
It stands to reason he must know about all 's
    worth a-knowin'!
So when a politician with a record 's on the
    track,
        We 're apt to hear some history
            From little Mack.

And when a fellow-journalist is broke and
    needs a twenty,
Who 's allus ready to whack up a portion
    of his plenty ?
Who 's allus got a wallet that 's as full of
    sordid gain
As his heart is full of kindness and his head
    is full of brain ?
Whose bowels of compassion will in-va-ri-a-
    bly move
Their owner to those courtesies which
    plainly, surely prove
That he 's the kind of person that never
    does go back
        On a fellow that 's in trouble ?
        Why, little Mack !

I 've heard 'em tell of Dana, and of Bonner,
    and of Reid,
Of Johnnie Cockerill, who, I 'll own, is very
    smart indeed;
Yet I don't care what their renown or in-
    fluence may be,
One metropolitan exchange is quite enough
    for me !

39

So keep your Danas, Bonners, Reids, your
    Cockerills, and the rest,
The woods is full of better men all through
    this woolly West;
For all that sleek, pretentious, Eastern edi-
    torial pack
        We would n't swap the shadow of
        Our little Mack!

TO ROBIN GOODFELLOW

I SEE you, Maister Bawsy-brown,
 Through yonder lattice creepin';
You come for cream and to gar me dream,
 But you dinna find me sleepin'.
The moonbeam, that upon the floor
 Wi' crickets ben a-jinkin',
Now steals away fra' her bonnie play —
 Wi' a rosier blie, I 'm thinkin'.

I saw you, Maister Bawsy-brown,
 When the blue bells went a-ringin'
For the merrie fays o' the banks an' braes,
 And I kenned your bonnie singin';
The gowans gave you honey sweets,
 And the posies on the heather
Dript draughts o' dew for the faery crew
 That danct and sang together.

41

But posie-bloom an' simmer-dew
    And ither sweets o' faery
C'u'd na gae down wi' Bawsy-brown,
    Sae nigh to Maggie's dairy!
My pantry shelves, sae clean and white,
    Are set wi' cream and cheeses,—
Gae, gin you will, an' take your fill
    Of whatsoever pleases.

Then wave your wand aboon my een
    Until they close awearie,
And the night be past sae sweet and fast
    Wi' dreamings o' my dearie.
But pinch the wench in yonder room,
    For she 's na gude nor bonnie,—
Her shelves be dust and her pans be rust,
    And she winkit at my Johnnie!

APPLE-PIE AND CHEESE

FULL many a sinful notion
  Conceived of foreign powers
Has come across the ocean
  To harm this land of ours;
And heresies called fashions
  Have modesty effaced,
And baleful, morbid passions
  Corrupt our native taste.
O tempora! O mores!
  What profanations these
That seek to dim the glories
  Of apple-pie and cheese!

I 'm glad my education
  Enables me to stand
Against the vile temptation
  Held out on every hand;
Eschewing all the tittles
  With vanity replete,

I 'm loyal to the victuals
  Our grandsires used to eat!
I 'm glad I 've got three willing boys
  To hang around and tease
Their mother for the filling joys
  Of apple-pie and cheese!

Your flavored creams and ices
  And your dainty angel-food
Aie mighty fine devices
  To regale the dainty dude;
Your terrapin and oysters,
  With wine to wash 'em down,
Are just the thing for roisters
  When painting of the town;
No flippant, sugared notion
  Shall *my* appetite appease,
Or bate my soul's devotion
  To apple-pie and cheese!

The pie my Julia makes me
  (God bless her Yankee ways!)
On memory's pinions takes me
  To dear Green Mountain days;

And seems like I see Mother
  Lean on the window-sill,
A-handin' me and brother
  What she knows 'll keep us still;
And these feelings are so grateful,
  Says I, "Julia, if you please,
I 'll take another plateful
  Of that apple-pie and cheese!"

And cheese! No alien it, sir,
  That 's brought across the sea, —
No Dutch antique, nor Switzer,
  Nor glutinous de Brie;
There 's nothing I abhor so
  As mawmets of this ilk —
Give *me* the harmless morceau
  That 's made of true-blue milk!
No matter what conditions
  Dyspeptic come to feaze,
The best of all physicians
  Is apple-pie and cheese!

Though ribalds may decry 'em,
  For these twin boons we stand,
Partaking thrice per diem
  Of their fulness out of hand;

45

No enervating fashion
  Shall cheat us of our right
To gratify our passion
  With a mouthful at a bite!
We 'll cut it square or bias,
  Or any way we please,
And faith shall justify us
  When we carve our pie and cheese!

De gustibus, 't is stated,
  Non disputandum est.
Which meaneth, when translated
  That all is for the best.
So let the foolish choose 'em
  The vapid sweets of sin,
I will not disabuse 'em
  Of the heresy they 're in;
But I, when I undress me
  Each night, upon my knees
Will ask the Lord to bless me
  With apple-pie and cheese!

KRINKEN

KRINKEN was a little child,—
It was summer when he smiled.
Oft the hoary sea and grim
Stretched its white arms out to him,
Calling, "Sun-child, come to me;
Let me warm my heart with thee!"
But the child heard not the sea,
Calling, yearning evermore
For the summer on the shore.

Krinken on the beach one day
Saw a maiden Nis at play;
On the pebbly beach she played
In the summer Krinken made.
Fair, and very fair, was she,
Just a little child was he.
"Krinken," said the maiden Nis,
"Let me have a little kiss,—

47

Just a kiss, and go with me
To the summer-lands that be
Down within the silver sea."

Krinken was a little child —
By the maiden Nis beguiled,
Hand in hand with her went he,
And 't was summer in the sea.
And the hoary sea and grim
To its bosom folded him —
Clasped and kissed the little form,
And the ocean's heart was warm.

Now the sea calls out no more;
It is winter on the shore, —
Winter where that little child
Made sweet summer when he smiled;
Though 't is summer on the sea
Where with maiden Nis went he, —
Summer, summer evermore, —
It is winter on the shore,
Winter, winter evermore.
Of the summer on the deep
Come sweet visions in my sleep:
His fair face lifts from the sea,
His dear voice calls out to me, —
These my dreams of summer be.

Krinken was a little child,
By the maiden Nis beguiled;
Oft the hoary sea and grim
Reached its longing arms to him,
Crying, "Sun-child, come to me;
Let me warm my heart with thee!"
But the sea calls out no more;
It is winter on the shore,—
Winter, cold and dark and wild;
Krinken was a little child,—
It was summer when he smiled;
Down he went into the sea,
And the winter bides with me.
Just a little child was he.

BÉRANGER'S "BROKEN FIDDLE"

I

THERE, there, poor dog, my faithful friend,
   Pay you no heed unto my sorrow:
But feast to-day while yet you may,—
   Who knows but we shall starve to-
     morrow!

II

"Give us a tune," the foemen cried,
   In one of their profane caprices;
I bade them "No"—they frowned, and, lo!
   They dashed this innocent in pieces!

III

This fiddle was the village pride—
   The mirth of every fête enhancing;
Its wizard art set every heart
   As well as every foot to dancing.

IV

How well the bridegroom knew its voice,
　　As from its strings its song went gushing!
Nor long delayed the promised maid
　　Equipped for bridal, coy and blushing.

V

Why, it discoursed so merrily,
　　It quickly banished all dejection;
And yet, when pressed, our priest confessed
　　I played with pious circumspection.

VI

And though, in patriotic song,
　　It was our guide, compatriot, teacher,
I never thought the foe had wrought
　　His fury on the helpless creature!

VII

But there, poor dog, my faithful friend,
　　Pay you no heed unto my sorrow;
I prithee take this paltry cake,—
　　Who knows but we shall starve to-
　　　morrow!

VIII

Ah, who shall lead the Sunday choir
　　As this old fiddle used to do it?
Can vintage come, with this voice dumb
　　That used to bid a welcome to it?

IX

It soothed the weary hours of toil,
　　It brought forgetfulness to debtors;
Time and again from wretched men
　　It struck oppression's galling fetters.

X

No man could hear its voice, and hate;
　　It stayed the teardrop at its portal;
With that dear thing I was a king
　　As never yet was monarch mortal!

XI

Now has the foe—the vandal foe—
　　Struck from my hands their pride and glory;
There let it lie!　In vengeance, I
　　Shall wield another weapon, gory!

XII

And if, O countrymen, I fall,
  Beside our grave let this be spoken:
"No foe of France shall ever dance
  Above the heart and fiddle, broken!"

XIII

So come, poor dog, my faithful friend,
  I prithee do not heed my sorrow,
But feast to-day while yet you may,
  For we are like to starve to-morrow.

THE LITTLE PEACH

A LITTLE peach in the orchard grew,—
A little peach of emerald hue;
Warmed by the sun and wet by the dew,
It grew.

One day, passing that orchard through,
That little peach dawned on the view
Of Johnny Jones and his sister Sue—
Them two.

Up at that peach a club they threw—
Down from the stem on which it grew
Fell that peach of emerald hue.
Mon Dieu!

John took a bite and Sue a chew,
And then the trouble began to brew,—
Trouble the doctor could n't subdue.
Too true!

Under the turf where the daisies grew
They planted John and his sister Sue,
And their little souls to the angels flew,—
    Boo hoo!

What of that peach of the emerald hue,
Warmed by the sun, and wet by the dew?
Ah, well, its mission on earth is through.
    Adieu!

1880.

HORACE III. 13

O FOUNTAIN of Bandusia,
  Whence crystal waters flow,
With garlands gay and wine I'll pay
  The sacrifice I owe;
A sportive kid with budding horns
  I have, whose crimson blood
Anon shall dye and sanctify
  Thy cool and babbling flood.

O fountain of Bandusia,
  The dog-star's hateful spell
No evil brings unto the springs
  That from thy bosom well;
Here oxen, wearied by the plough,
  The roving cattle here,
Hasten in quest of certain rest
  And quaff thy gracious cheer.

O fountain of Bandusia,
　　Ennobled shalt thou be,
For I shall sing the joys that spring
　　Beneath yon ilex-tree;
Yes, fountain of Bandusia,
　　Posterity shall know
The cooling brooks that from thy nooks
　　Singing and dancing go!

THE DIVINE LULLABY

I HEAR Thy voice, dear Lord;
  I hear it by the stormy sea
  When winter nights are black and wild,
And when, affright, I call to Thee;
It calms my fears and whispers me,
  "Sleep well, my child."

  I hear Thy voice, dear Lord,
In singing winds, in falling snow,
  The curfew chimes, the midnight bell.
"Sleep well, my child," it murmurs low;
"The guardian angels come and go,—
  O child, sleep well!"

  I hear Thy voice, dear Lord,
Ay, though the singing winds be stilled,
  Though hushed the tumult of the deep,

My fainting heart with anguish chilled
By Thy assuring tone is thrilled,—
  "Fear not, and sleep!"

  Speak on — speak on, dear Lord!
And when the last dread night is near,
  With doubts and fears and terrors wild,
Oh, let my soul expiring hear
Only these words of heavenly cl.eer,
  "Sleep well, my child!"

IN THE FIRELIGHT

THE fire upon the hearth is low,
  And there is stillness everywhere,
  While like winged spirits, here and there,
The firelight shadows fluttering go.
And as the shadows round me creep,
  A childish treble breaks the gloom,
  And softly from a further room
Comes, "Now I lay me down to sleep."

And somehow, with that little prayer
  And that sweet treble in my ears,
  My thoughts go back to distant years
And linger with a loved one there;
And as I hear my child's amen,
  My mother's faith comes back to me,—
  Crouched at her side I seem to be,
And Mother holds my hands again.

Oh, for an hour in that dear place!
  Oh, for the peace of that dear time!
  Oh, for that childish trust sublime!
Oh, for a glimpse of Mother's face!
Yet, as the shadows round me creep,
  I do not seem to be alone,—
  Sweet magic of that treble tone,
And "Now I lay me down to sleep."

1885.

HEINE'S "WIDOW OR DAUGHTER?"

SHALL I woo the one or other?
  Both attract me — more's the pity!
Pretty is the widowed mother,
  And the daughter, too, is pretty.

When I see that maiden shrinking,
  By the gods I swear I 'll get 'er!
But anon I fall to thinking
  That the mother 'll suit me better!

So, like any idiot ass
  Hungry for the fragrant fodder,
Placed between two bales of grass,
  Lo, I doubt, delay, and dodder!

CHRISTMAS TREASURES

I COUNT my treasures o'er with care.—
  The little toy my darling knew,
  A little sock of faded hue,
A little lock of golden hair.

Long years ago this holy time,
  My little one — my all to me —
  Sat robed in white upon my knee
And heard the merry Christmas chime.

"Tell me, my little golden-head,
  If Santa Claus should come to-night,
  What shall he bring my baby bright,—
What treasure for my boy?" I said.

And then he named this little toy,
  While in his round and mournful eyes
  There came a look of sweet surprise,
That spake his quiet, trustful joy.

And as he lisped his evening prayer
  He asked the boon with childish grace;
  Then, toddling to the chimney-place,
He hung this little stocking there.

That night, while lengthening shadows crept,
  I saw the white-winged angels come
  With singing to our lowly home
And kiss my darling as he slept.

They must have heard his little prayer,
  For in the morn, with rapturous face,
  He toddled to the chimney-place,
And found this little treasure there.

They came again one Christmas-tide,—
  That angel host, so fair and white!
  And singing all that glorious night,
They lured my darling from my side.

A little sock, a little toy,
  A little lock of golden hair,
  The Christmas music on the air,
A watching for my baby boy!

But if again that angel train
   And golden-head come back for me,
   To bear me to Eternity,
My watching will not be in vain!

1879.

DE AMICITIIS

THOUGH care and strife
    Elsewhere be rife,
Upon my word I do not heed 'em;
    In bed I lie
    With books hard by,
And with increasing zest I read 'em.

    Propped up in bed,
    So much I 've read
Of musty tomes that I 've a headful
    Of tales and rhymes
    Of ancient times,
Which, wife declares, are "simply dreadful!"

    They give me joy
    Without alloy;
And is n't that what books are made for?
    And yet — and yet —
    (Ah, vain regret!)
I would to God they all were paid for!

No festooned cup
Filled foaming up
Can lure me elsewhere to confound me;
Sweeter than wine
This love of mine
For these old books I see around me!

A plague, I say,
On maidens gay;
I 'll weave no compliments to tell 'em!
Vain fool I were,
Did I prefer
Those dolls to these old friends in vellum!

At dead of night
My chamber 's bright
Not only with the gas that 's burning,
But with the glow
Of long ago,—
Of beauty back from eld returning.

Fair women's looks
I see in books,
I see *them,* and I hear their laughter,—
Proud, high-born maids,
Unlike the jades
Which men-folk now go chasing after!

Herein again
Speak valiant men
Of all nativities and ages;
I hear and smile
With rapture while
I turn these musty, magic pages.

The sword, the lance,
The morris dance,
The highland song, the greenwood ditty,
Of these I read,
Or, when the need,
My Miller grinds me grist that 's gritty!

When of such stuff
We 've had enough,
Why, there be other friends to greet us;
We 'll moralize
In solemn wise
With Plato or with Epictetus.

Sneer as you may,
I 'm proud to say
That I, for one, am very grateful
To Heaven, that sends
These genial friends
To banish other friendships hateful!

And when I 'm done,
I 'd have no son
Pounce on these treasures like a vulture;
Nay, give them half
My epitaph,
And let them share in my sepulture.

Then, when the crack
Of doom rolls back
The marble and the earth that hide me,
I 'll smuggle home
Each precious tome,
Without a fear my wife shall chide me!

OUR LADY OF THE MINE

THE Blue Horizon wuz a mine us fellers
   all thought well uv,
And there befell the episode I now perpose
   to tell uv;
'T wuz in the year uv sixty-nine,— some-
   where along in summer,—
There hove in sight one afternoon a new
   and curious comer;
His name wuz Silas Pettibone,— a' artist by
   perfession,—
With a kit of tools and a big mustache and
   a pipe in his possession.
He told us, by our leave, he 'd kind uv like
   to make some sketches
Uv the snowy peaks, 'nd the foamin' crick,
   'nd the distant mountain stretches;
"You 're welkim, sir," sez we, although
   this scenery dodge seemed to us
A waste uv time where scenery wuz already
   sooper-*floo*-us.

All through the summer Pettibone kep' busy
　　at his sketchin',—
At daybreak off for Eagle Pass, and home at
　　nightfall, fetchin'
That everlastin' book uv his with spider-lines
　　all through it;
Three-Fingered Hoover used to say there
　　war n't no meanin' to it.
"Gol durn a man," sez he to him, "whose
　　shif'less hand is sot at
A-drawin' hills that 's full uv quartz that 's
　　pinin' to be got at!"
"Go on," sez Pettibone, "go on, if joshin'
　　gratifies ye;
But one uv these fine times I 'll show ye
　　sumthin' will surprise ye!"
The which remark led us to think — although
　　he did n't say it —
That Pettibone wuz owin' us a gredge 'nd
　　meant to pay it.

One evenin' as we sat around the Restauraw
　　de Casey,
A-singin' songs 'nd tellin' yarns the which
　　wuz sumwhat racy,

71

In come that feller Pettibone, 'nd sez, "With
    your permission,
I 'd like to put a picture I have made on ex-
    hibition."
He sot the picture on the bar 'nd drew aside
    its curtain,
Sayin', "I reckon you'll allow as how *that's*
    art, f'r certain!"
And then we looked, with jaws agape, but
    nary word wuz spoken,
And f'r a likely spell the charm uv silence
    wuz unbroken —
Till presently, as in a dream, remarked Three-
    Fingered Hoover:
"Onless I am mistaken, this is Pettibone's
    shef doover!"

It wuz a face — a human face — a woman's,
    fair 'nd tender —
Sot gracefully upon a neck white as a swan's,
    and slender;
The hair wuz kind uv sunny, 'nd the eyes
    wuz sort uv dreamy,
The mouth wuz half a-smilin', 'nd the cheeks
    wuz soft 'nd creamy;

It seemed like she wuz lookin' off into the
    west out yonder,
And seemed like, while she looked, we saw
    her eyes grow softer, fonder,—
Like, lookin' off into the west, where moun-
    tain mists wuz fallin',
She saw the face she longed to see and heerd
    his voice a-callin';
"Hooray!" we cried,— "a woman in the
    camp uv Blue Horizon!
Step right up, Colonel Pettibone, 'nd nomi-
    nate your pizen!"

A curious situation,— one deservin' uv your
    pity,—
No human, livin', female thing this side of
    Denver City!
But jest a lot uv husky men that lived on
    sand 'nd bitters,—
Do you wonder that that woman's face con-
    soled the lonesome critters?
And not a one but what it served in some
    way to remind him
Of a mother or a sister or a sweetheart left
    behind him;

And some looked back on happier days, and
    saw the old-time faces
And heerd the dear familiar sounds in old
    familiar places,—
A gracious touch of home. "Look here," sez
    Hoover, "ever'body
Quit thinkin' 'nd perceed at oncet to name
    his favorite toddy!"

It wuz n't long afore the news had spread
    the country over,
And miners come a-flockin' in like honey-
    bees to clover;
It kind uv did 'em good, they said, to feast
    their hungry eyes on
That picture uv Our Lady in the camp uv
    Blue Horizon.
But one mean cuss from Nigger Crick passed
    criticisms on 'er,—
Leastwise we overheerd him call her Petti-
    bone's madonner,
The which we did not take to be respectful
    to a lady,
So we hung him in a quiet spot that wuz
    cool 'nd dry 'nd shady;

Which same might not have been good law,
    but it *wuʒ* the right manœuvre
To give the critics due respect for Petti-
    bone's shef doover.

Gone is the camp,—yes, years ago the Blue
    Horizon busted,
And every mother's son uv us got up one
    day 'nd dusted,
While Pettibone perceeded East with wealth
    in his possession,
And went to Yurrup, as I heerd, to study
    his perfession;
So, like as not, you 'll find him now a-paint-
    in' heads 'nd faces
At Venus, Billy Florence, and the like I-tal-
    yun places.
But no sech face he 'll paint again as at old
    Blue Horizon,
For I 'll allow no sweeter face no human
    soul sot eyes on;
And when the critics talk so grand uv Paris
    'nd the Loover,
I say, "Oh, but you orter seen the Petti-
    bone shef doover!"

THE WANDERER

UPON a mountain height, far from the
sea,
　　I found a shell,
And to my listening ear the lonely thing
Ever a song of ocean seemed to sing,
　　Ever a tale of ocean seemed to tell.

How came the shell upon that mountain
　　height?
　　Ah, who can say
Whether there dropped by some too careless
　　hand,
Or whether there cast when Ocean swept
　　the Land,
　　Ere the Eternal had ordained the Day?

Strange, was it not? Far from its native
      deep,
    One song it sang,—
Sang of the awful mysteries of the tide,
Sang of the misty sea, profound and wide,—
    Ever with echoes of the ocean rang.

And as the shell upon the mountain height
    Sings of the sea,
So do I ever, leagues and leagues away,—
So do I ever, wandering where I may,—
    Sing, O my home! sing, O my home!
      of thee.

1883.

TO A USURPER

AHA! a traitor in the camp,
   A rebel strangely bold,—
A lisping, laughing, toddling scamp,
   Not more than four years old!

To think that I, who 've ruled alone
   So proudly in the past,
Should be ejected from my throne
   By my own son at last!

He trots his treason to and fro,
   As only babies can,
And says he 'll be his mamma's beau
   When he 's a "gweat, big man"!

You stingy boy! you 've always had
   A share in mamma's heart;
Would you begrudge your poor old dad
   The tiniest little part?

That mamma, I regret to see,
    Inclines to take your part,—
As if a dual monarchy
    Should rule her gentle heart!

But when the years of youth have sped,
    The bearded man, I trow,
Will quite forget he ever said
    He 'd be his mamma's beau.

Renounce your treason, little son,
    Leave mamma's heart to me;
For there will come another one
    To claim your loyalty.

And when that other comes to you,
    God grant her love may shine
Through all your life, as fair and true
    As mamma's does through mine!

1885.

LULLABY; BY THE SEA

FAIR is the castle up on the hill —
    Hushaby, sweet my own!
The night is fair, and the waves are still,
And the wind is singing to you and to me
In this lowly home beside the sea —
    Hushaby, sweet my own!

On yonder hill is store of wealth —
    Hushaby, sweet my own!
And revellers drink to a little one's health;
But you and I bide night and day
For the other love that has sailed away —
    Hushaby, sweet my own!

See not, dear eyes, the forms that creep
    Ghostlike, O my own!
Out of the mists of the murmuring deep;

Oh, see them not and make no cry
Till the angels of death have passed us by—
    Hushaby, sweet my own!

Ah, little they reck of you and me—
    Hushaby, sweet my own!
In our lonely home beside the sea;
They seek the castle up on the hill,
And there they will do their ghostly will—
    Hushaby, O my own!

Here by the sea a mother croons
    "Hushaby, sweet my own!"
In yonder castle a mother swoons
While the angels go down to the misty deep,
Bearing a little one fast asleep—
    Hushaby, sweet my own!

SOLDIER, MAIDEN, AND FLOWER

"SWEETHEART, take this," a soldier said,
    " And bid me brave good-by;
It may befall we ne'er shall wed,
    But love can never die.
Be steadfast in thy troth to me,
    And then, whate'er my lot,
'My soul to God, my heart to thee,'—
    Sweetheart, forget me not!"

The maiden took the tiny flower
    And nursed it with her tears:
Lo! he who left her in that hour
    Came not in after years.
Unto a hero's death he rode
    'Mid shower of fire and shot;
But in the maiden's heart abode
    The flower, forget-me-not.

And when *he* came not with the rest
    From out the years of blood,
Closely unto her widowed breast
    She pressed a faded bud;
Oh, there is love and there is pain,
    And there is peace, God wot,—
And these dear three do live again
    In sweet forget-me-not.

'T is to an unmarked grave to-day
    That I should love to go,—
Whether he wore the blue or gray,
    What need that we should know?
"He loved a woman," let us say,
    And on that sacred spot,
To woman's love, that lives for aye,
    We 'll strew forget-me-not.

1887.

HORACE TO MELPOMENE

LOFTY and enduring is the monument
  I 've reared,—
    Come, tempests, with your bitterness as-
      sailing;
And thou, corrosive blasts of time, by all
    things mortal feared,
    Thy buffets and thy rage are unavailing!

I shall not altogether die; by far my greater
    part
    Shall mock man's common fate in realms
      infernal;
My works shall live as tributes to my genius
    and my art,—
    My works shall be my monument eternal!

While this great Roman empire stands and
    gods protect our fanes,
  Mankind with grateful hearts shall tell the
    story,
How one most lowly born upon the parched
    Apulian plains
  First raised the native lyric muse to glory.

Assume, revered Melpomene, the proud es-
    tate I 've won,
  And, with thine own dear hand the meed
    supplying,
Bind thou about the forehead of thy cele-
    brated son
  The Delphic laurel-wreath of fame un-
    dying!

AILSIE, MY BAIRN

LIE in my arms, Ailsie, my bairn,—
   Lie in my arms and dinna greit;
Long time been past syn I kenned you last,
   But my harte been allwais the same, my
      swete.

Ailsie, I colde not say you ill,
   For out of the mist of your bitter tears,
And the prayers that rise from your bonnie
      eyes
   Cometh a promise of oder yeres.

I mind the time when we lost our bairn,—
   Do you ken that time ? A wambling tot,
You wandered away ane simmer day,
   And we hunted and called, and found you
      not.

I promised God, if He 'd send you back,
   Alwaies to keepe and to love you, childe;
And I 'm thinking again of that promise when
   I see you creep out of the storm sae wild.

You came back then as you come back
   now,—
   Your kirtle torn and your face all white;
And you stood outside and knockit and cried,
   Just as you, dearie, did to-night.

Oh, never a word of the cruel wrang,
   That has faded your cheek and dimmed
      your ee;
And never a word of the fause, fause lord,—
   Only a smile and a kiss for me.

Lie in my arms, as long, long syne,
   And sleepe on my bosom, deere wounded
      thing,—
I 'm nae sae glee as I used to be,
   Or I 'd sing you the songs I used to sing.

But Ile kemb my fingers thro' y'r haire,
   And nane shall know, but you and I,
Of the love and the faith that came to us baith
   When Ailsie, my bairn, came home to die.

CORNISH LULLABY

OUT on the mountain over the town,
   All night long, all night long,
The trolls go up and the trolls go down,
   Bearing their packs and crooning a song;
And this is the song the hill-folk croon,
As they trudge in the light of the misty
    moon,—
This is ever their dolorous tune:
"Gold, gold! ever more gold,—
    Bright red gold for dearie!"

Deep in the hill the yeoman delves
   All night long, all night long;
None but the peering, furtive elves
   See his toil and hear his song;
Merrily ever the cavern rings
As merrily ever his pick he swings,
And merrily ever this song he sings:
"Gold, gold! ever more gold,—
    Bright red gold for dearie!"

88

Mother is rocking thy lowly bed
   All night long, all night long,
Happy to smooth thy curly head
   And to hold thy hand and to sing her song;
'T is not of the hill-folk, dwarfed and old,
Nor the song of the yeoman, stanch and bold,
And the burden it beareth is not of gold;
But it 's "Love, love!—nothing but love,—
     Mother's love for dearie!"

UHLAND'S "THREE CAVALIERS"

THERE were three cavaliers that went
over the Rhine,
And gayly they called to the hostess for
wine.
"And where is thy daughter? We would
she were here,—
Go fetch us that maiden to gladden our
cheer!"

"I 'll fetch thee thy goblets full foaming,"
she said,
"But in yon darkened chamber the maiden
lies dead."
And lo! as they stood in the doorway, the
white
Of a shroud and a dead shrunken face met
their sight.

Then the first cavalier breathed a pitiful sigh,
And the throb of his heart seemed to melt
in his eye,
And he cried, "Hadst thou lived, O my
pretty white rose,
I ween I had loved thee and wed thee —
who knows?"

The next cavalier drew aside a small space,
And stood to the wall with his hands to his
face;
And this was the heart-cry that came with
his tears:
"I loved her, I loved her these many long
years!"

But the third cavalier kneeled him down in
that place,
And, as it were holy, he kissed that dead
face:
"I loved thee long years, and I love thee
to-day,
And I'll love thee, dear maiden, forever and
aye!"

A CHAUCERIAN PARAPHRASE OF
HORACE

SYN that you, Chloe, to your moder
sticken,
Maketh all ye yonge bacheloures full sicken;
Like as a lyttel deere you ben y-hiding
Whenas come lovers with theyre pityse
chiding;
Sothly it ben faire to give up your moder
For to beare swete company with some
oder;
Your moder ben well enow so farre shee
goeth,
But that ben not farre enow, God knoweth;
Wherefore it ben sayed that foolysh ladyes
That marrye not shall leade an aype in
Hadys;
But all that do with gode men wed full
quickylye
When that they be on dead go to ye seints
full sickerly.

NORSE LULLABY

THE sky is dark and the hills are white
   As the storm-king speeds from the
      north to-night,
And this is the song the storm-king sings,
As over the world his cloak he flings:
   "Sleep, sleep, little one, sleep;"
He rustles his wings and gruffly sings:
   "Sleep, little one, sleep."

On yonder mountain-side a vine
Clings at the foot of a mother pine;
The tree bends over the trembling thing,
And only the vine can hear her sing:
   "Sleep, sleep, little one, sleep;
What shall you fear when I am here?
   Sleep, little one, sleep."

The king may sing in his bitter flight,
The tree may croon to the vine to-night,
But the little snowflake at my breast
Liketh the song *I* sing the best,—
　　Sleep, sleep, little one, sleep;
Weary thou art, anext my heart
　　Sleep, little one, sleep.

BÉRANGER'S "MY LAST SONG PERHAPS"

[JANUARY, 1814]

WHEN, to despoil my native France,
 With flaming torch and cruel sword
And boisterous drums her foeman comes,
 I curse him and his vandal horde!
Yet, what avail accrues to her,
 If we assume the garb of woe?
Let 's merry be,— in laughter we
 May rescue somewhat from the foe!

Ah, many a brave man trembles now.
 I (coward!) show no sign of fear;
When Bacchus sends his blessing, friends,
 I drown my panic in his cheer.
Come, gather round my humble board,
 And let the sparkling wassail flow,—
Chuckling to think, the while you drink,
 "This much we rescue from the foe!"

My creditors beset me so
   And so environed my abode,
That I agreed, despite my need,
   To settle up the debts I owed;
When suddenly there came the news
   Of this invasion, as you know;
I 'll pay no score; pray, lend me more,—
   I— *I* will keep it from the foe!

Now here 's my mistress,— pretty dear!—
   Feigns terror at this martial noise,
And yet, methinks, the artful minx
   Would like to meet those soldier boys!
I tell her that they 're coarse and rude,
   Yet feel she don't believe 'em so,—
Well, never mind; so she be kind,
   That much I rescue from the foe!

If, brothers, hope shall have in store
   For us and ours no friendly glance,
Let 's rather die than raise a cry
   Of welcome to the foes of France!
But, like the swan that dying sings,
   Let us, O Frenchmen, singing go,—
Then shall our cheer, when death is near,
   Be so much rescued from the foe!

MR. DANA, OF THE NEW YORK SUN

THAR showed up out'n Denver in the
    spring uv '81
A man who 'd worked with Dana on the
    Noo York Sun.
His name wuz Cantell Whoppers, 'nd he
    wuz a sight ter view
Ez he walked inter the orfice 'nd inquired
    fer work ter do.
Thar war n't no places vacant then,— fer be
    it understood,
That wuz the time when talent flourished at
    that altitood;
But thar the stranger lingered, tellin' Ray-
    mond 'nd the rest
Uv what perdigious wonders he could do
    when at his best,
Till finally he stated (quite by chance) that
    he hed done
A heap uv work with Dana on the Noo York
    Sun.

Wall, that wuz quite another thing; we
    owned that ary cuss
Who 'd worked f'r Mr. Dana *must* be good
    enough fer *us !*
And so we tuk the stranger's word 'nd nipped
    him while we could,
For if *we did n't* take him we knew John
    Arkins *would;*
And Cooper, too, wuz mouzin' round fer
    enterprise 'nd brains,
Whenever them commodities blew in across
    the plains.
At any rate we nailed him, which made ol'
    Cooper swear
And Arkins tear out handfuls uv his copious
    curly hair;
But *we* set back and cackled, 'nd hed a power
    uv fun
With our man who 'd worked with Dana
    on the Noo York Sun.

It made our eyes hang on our cheeks 'nd
    lower jaws ter drop,
Ter hear that feller tellin' how ol' Dana run
    his shop:

It seems that Dana wuz the biggest man you
    ever saw,—
He lived on human bein's, 'nd preferred to
    eat 'em raw!
If he hed Democratic drugs ter take, before he
    took 'em,
As good old allopathic laws prescribe, he allus
    shook 'em.
The man that could set down 'nd write like
    Dany never grew,
And the sum of human knowledge wuz n't
    half what Dana knew;
The consequence appeared to be that nearly
    every one
Concurred with Mr. Dana of the Noo York
    Sun.

This feller, Cantell Whoppers, never brought
    an item in,—
He spent his time at Perrin's shakin' poker
    dice f'r gin.
Whatever the assignment, he wuz allus sure
    to shirk,
He wuz very long on likker and all-fired
    short on work!

If any other cuss had played the tricks he
    dared ter play,
The daisies would be bloomin' over his re-
    mains to-day;
But somehow folks respected him and stood
    him to the last,
Considerin' his superior connections in the
    past.
So, when he bilked at poker, not a sucker
    drew a gun
On the man who 'd worked with Dana on
    the Noo York Sun.

Wall, Dana came ter Denver in the fall uv
    '83,
A very different party from the man we
    thought ter see,—
A nice 'nd clean old gentleman, so dignerfied
    'nd calm,
You bet yer life he never did no human
    bein' harm!
A certain hearty manner 'nd a fulness uv
    the vest
Betokened that his sperrits 'nd his victuals
    wuz the best;

His face wuz so benevolent, his smile so
    sweet 'nd kind,
That they seemed to be the reflex uv an
    honest, healthy mind;
And God had set upon his head a crown uv
    silver hair
In promise uv the golden crown He meaneth
    him to wear.
So, uv us boys that met him out'n Denver,
    there wuz none
But fell in love with Dana uv the Noo York
    Sun.

But when he came to Denver in that fall
    uv '83,
His old friend Cantell Whoppers disappeared
    upon a spree;
The very thought uv seein' Dana worked
    upon him so
(They had n't been together fer a year or
    two, you know),
That he borrered all the stuff he could and
    started on a bat,
And, strange as it may seem, we did n't
    see him after that.

So, when ol' Dana hove in sight, we could
    n't understand
Why he did n't seem to notice that his crony
    wa'n't on hand;
No casual allusion, not a question, no, not
    one,
For the man who 'd "worked with Dana
    on the Noo York Sun!"

We broke it gently to him, but he did n't
    seem surprised,
Thar wuz no big burst uv passion as we
    fellers had surmised.
He said that Whoppers wuz a man he 'd
    never heerd about,
But he mought have carried papers on a
    Jarsey City route;
And then he recollected hearin' Mr. Laffan
    say
That he 'd fired a man named Whoppers fur
    bein' drunk one day,
Which, with more likker *underneath* than
    money *in* his vest,
Had started on a freight-train fur the great
    'nd boundin' West,

But further information or statistics he had
none
Uv the man who 'd "worked with Dana on
the Noo York Sun."

We dropped the matter quietly 'nd never
made no fuss,—
When we get played for suckers, why, that's
a horse on us!—
But every now 'nd then we Denver fellers
have to laff
To hear some other paper boast uv havin' on
its staff
A man who 's "worked with Dana," 'nd
then we fellers wink
And pull our hats down on our eyes 'nd set
around 'nd think.
It seems like Dana could n't be as smart as
people say,
If he educates so many folks 'nd lets 'em get
away;
And, as for us, in future we 'll be very apt
to shun
The man who "worked with Dana on the
Noo York Sun."

But bless ye, Mr. Dana! may you live a
    thousan' years,
To sort o' keep things lively in this vale of
    human tears;
An' may *I* live a thousan', too,—a thousan'
    less a day,
For I should n't like to be on earth to hear
    you 'd passed away.
And when it comes your time to go you 'll
    need no Latin chaff
Nor biographic data put in your epitaph;
But one straight line of English and of truth
    will let folks know
The homage 'nd the gratitude 'nd reverence
    they owe;
You 'll need no epitaph but this: "Here
    sleeps the man who run
That best 'nd brightest paper, the Noo York
    Sun."

SICILIAN LULLABY

HUSH, little one, and fold your hands;
The sun hath set, the moon is high;
The sea is singing to the sands,
And wakeful posies are beguiled
By many a fairy lullaby:
Hush, little child, my little child!

Dream, little one, and in your dreams
Float upward from this lowly place, —
Float out on mellow, misty streams
To lands where bideth Mary mild,
And let her kiss thy little face,
You little child, my little child!

Sleep, little one, and take thy rest,
With angels bending over thee, —
Sleep sweetly on that Father's breast
Whom our dear Christ hath reconciled;
But stay not there, — come back to me,
O little child, my little child!

HORACE TO PYRRHA

WHAT perfumed, posie-dizened sirrah,
  With smiles for diet,
Clasps you, O fair but faithless Pyrrha,
  On the quiet?
For whom do you bind up your tresses,
  As spun-gold yellow,—
Meshes that go, with your caresses,
  To snare a fellow?

How will he rail at fate capricious,
  And curse you duly!
Yet now he deems your wiles delicious,
  You perfect, truly!
Pyrrha, your love 's a treacherous ocean;
  He 'll soon fall in there!
Then shall I gloat on his commotion,
  For *I* have been there!

THE TWENTY-THIRD PSALM

MY Shepherd is the Lord my God,—
  There is no want I know;
His flock He leads in verdant meads,
  Where tranquil waters flow.

He doth restore my fainting soul
  With His divine caress,
And, when I stray, He points the way
  To paths of righteousness.

Yea, though I walk the vale of death,
  What evil shall I fear?
Thy staff and rod are mine, O God,
  And Thou, my Shepherd, near!

Mine enemies behold the feast
  Which my dear Lord hath spread;
And, lo! my cup He filleth up,
  With oil anoints my head!

Goodness and mercy shall be mine
    Unto my dying day;
Then will I bide at His dear side
    Forever and for aye!

THE BIBLIOMANIAC'S BRIDE

THE women-folk are like to books,—
  Most pleasing to the eye,
Whereon if anybody looks
  He feels disposed to buy.

I hear that many are for sale,—
  Those that record no dates,
And such editions as regale
  The view with colored plates.

Of every quality and grade
  And size they may be found,—
Quite often beautifully made,
  As often poorly bound.

Now, as for me, had I my choice,
  I 'd choose no folio tall,
But some octavo to rejoice
  My sight and heart withal,—

As plump and pudgy as a snipe;
    Well worth her weight in gold;
Of honest, clean, conspicuous type,
    And *just* the size to hold!

With such a volume for my wife
    How should I keep and con!
How like a dream should run my life
    Unto its colophon!

Her frontispiece should be more fair
    Than any colored plate;
Blooming with health, she would not care
    To extra-illustrate.

And in her pages there should be
    A wealth of prose and verse,
With now and then a *jeu d'esprit,*—
    But nothing ever worse!

Prose for me when I wished for prose,
    Verse when to verse inclined,—
Forever bringing sweet repose
    To body, heart, and mind.

Oh, I should bind this priceless prize
   In bindings full and fine,
And keep her where no human eyes
   Should see her charms, but mine!

With such a fair unique as this
   What happiness abounds!
Who—who could paint my rapturous bliss,
   My joy unknown to Lowndes!

CHRISTMAS HYMN

SING, Christmas bells!
    Say to the earth this is the morn
Whereon our Saviour-King is born;
  Sing to all men,—the bond, the free,
The rich, the poor, the high, the low,
  The little child that sports in glee,
The aged folk that tottering go,—
    Proclaim the morn
    That Christ is born,
That saveth them and saveth me!

    Sing, angel host!
Sing of the star that God has placed
Above the manger in the east;
  Sing of the glories of the night,
The virgin's sweet humility,
  The Babe with kingly robes bedight,—

Sing to all men where'er they be
    This Christmas morn;
    For Christ is born,
That saveth them and saveth me!

    Sing, sons of earth!
O ransomed seed of Adam, sing!
God liveth, and we have a king!
    The curse is gone, the bond are free,—
By Bethlehem's star that brightly beamed,
    By all the heavenly signs that be,
We know that Israel is redeemed;
      That on this morn
      The Christ is born
    That saveth you and saveth me!

    Sing, O my heart!
Sing thou in rapture this dear morn
Whereon the blessed Prince is born!
    And as thy songs shall be of love,
So let my deeds be charity,—
    By the dear Lord that reigns above,
By Him that died upon the tree,
      By this fair morn
      Whereon is born
    The Christ that saveth all and me!

JAPANESE LULLABY

SLEEP, little pigeon, and fold your
wings,—
   Little blue pigeon with velvet eyes;
Sleep to the singing of mother-bird swing-
      ing —
   Swinging the nest where her little one lies.

Away out yonder I see a star,—
   Silvery star with a tinkling song;
To the soft dew falling I hear it calling —
   Calling and tinkling the night along.

In through the window a moonbeam
   comes,—
   Little gold moonbeam with misty wings;
All silently creeping, it asks, "Is he sleeping—
   Sleeping and dreaming while mother
      sings?"

Up from the sea there floats the sob
  Of the waves that are breaking upon the
    shore,
As though they were groaning in anguish,
    and moaning —
  Bemoaning the ship that shall come no
    more.

But sleep, little pigeon, and fold your
    wings, —
  Little blue pigeon with mournful eyes;
Am I not singing? — see, I am swinging —
  Swinging the nest where my darling lies.

"GOOD-BY — GOD BLESS YOU!"

I LIKE the Anglo-Saxon speech
   With its direct revealings;
It takes a hold, and seems to reach
   'Way down into your feelings;
That some folk deem it rude, I know,
   And therefore they abuse it;
But I have never found it so,—
   Before all else I choose it.
I don't object that men should air
   The Gallic they have paid for,
With "Au revoir," "Adieu, ma chère,"
   For that 's what French was made for.
But when a crony takes your hand
   At parting, to address you,
He drops all foreign lingo and
   He says, "Good-by—God bless you!"

This seems to me a sacred phrase,
   With reverence impassioned,—
A thing come down from righteous days,
   Quaintly but nobly fashioned;
It well becomes an honest face,
   A voice that 's round and cheerful;
It stays the sturdy in his place,
   And soothes the weak and fearful.
Into the porches of the ears
   It steals with subtle unction,
And in your heart of hearts appears
   To work its gracious function;
And all day long with pleasing song
   It lingers to caress you,—
I 'm sure no human heart goes wrong
   That 's told "Good-by—God bless
     you!"

I love the words,—perhaps because,
   When I was leaving Mother,
Standing at last in solemn pause
   We looked at one another,
And I—I saw in Mother's eyes
   The love she could not tell me,—
A love eternal as the skies,
   Whatever fate befell me;

She put her arms about my neck
    And soothed the pain of leaving,
And though her heart was like to break,
    She spoke no word of grieving;
She let no tear bedim her eye,
    For fear *that* might distress me,
But, kissing me, she said good-by,
    And asked our God to bless me.

HORACE TO PHYLLIS

COME, Phyllis, I 've a cask of wine
    That fairly reeks with precious juices,
And in your tresses you shall twine
    The loveliest flowers this vale produces.

My cottage wears a gracious smile,—
    The altar, decked in floral glory,
Yearns for the lamb which bleats the while
    As though it pined for honors gory.

Hither our neighbors nimbly fare,—
    The boys agog, the maidens snickering;
And savory smells possess the air
    As skyward kitchen flames are flickering.

You ask what means this grand display,
    This festive throng, and goodly diet?
Well, since you 're bound to have your way,
    I don't mind telling, on the quiet.

'T is April 13, as you know,—
    A day and month devote to Venus,
Whereon was born, some years ago,
    My very worthy friend Mæcenas.

Nay, pay no heed to Telephus,—
    Your friends agree he does n't love you;
The way he flirts convinces us
    He really is not worthy of you!

Aurora's son, unhappy lad!
    You know the fate that overtook him?
And Pegasus a rider had—
    I say he *had* before he shook him!

Hæc docet (as you must agree):
    'T is meet that Phyllis should discover
A wisdom in preferring me
    And mittening every other lover.

So come, O Phyllis, last and best
    Of loves with which this heart 's been
        smitten,—
Come, sing my jealous fears to rest,
    And let your songs be those *I 've* written.

CHRYSTMASSE OF OLDE

GOD rest you, Chrysten gentil men,
  Wherever you may be,—
God rest you all in fielde or hall,
  Or on ye stormy sea;
For on this morn oure Chryst is born
  That saveth you and me.

Last night ye shepherds in ye east
  Saw many a wondrous thing;
Ye sky last night flamed passing bright
  Whiles that ye stars did sing,
And angels came to bless ye name
  Of Jesus Chryst, oure Kyng.

God rest you, Chrysten gentil men,
  Faring where'er you may;
In noblesse court do thou no sport,
  In tournament no playe,
In paynim lands hold thou thy hands
  From bloudy works this daye.

But thinking on ye gentil Lord
    That died upon ye tree,
Let troublings cease and deeds of peace
    Abound in Chrystantie;
For on this morn ye Chryst is born
    That saveth you and me.

AT THE DOOR

I THOUGHT myself indeed secure,
  So fast the door, so firm the lock;
But, lo! he toddling comes to lure
  My parent ear with timorous knock.

My heart were stone could it withstand
  The sweetness of my baby's plea,—
That timorous, baby knocking and
  "Please let me in,—it 's only me."

I threw aside the unfinished book,
  Regardless of its tempting charms,
And opening wide the door, I took
  My laughing darling in my arms.

Who knows but in Eternity,
  I, like a truant child, shall wait
The glories of a life to be,
  Beyond the Heavenly Father's gate?

And will that Heavenly Father heed
  The truant's supplicating cry,
As at the outer door I plead,
  "'T is I, O Father! only I"?

1886.

HI-SPY

STRANGE that the city thoroughfare,
  Noisy and bustling all the day,
Should with the night renounce its care,
  And lend itself to children's play!

Oh, girls are girls, and boys are boys,
  And have been so since Abel's birth,
And shall be so till dolls and toys
  Are with the children swept from earth.

The self-same sport that crowns the day
  Of many a Syrian shepherd's son,
Beguiles the little lads at play
  By night in stately Babylon.

I hear their voices in the street,
  Yet 't is so different now from then!
Come, brother! from your winding-sheet,
  And let us two be boys again!

1886.

LITTLE CROODLIN DOO

HO, pretty bee, did you see my croodlin
doo?
　Ho, little lamb, is she jinkin' on the lea?
　Ho, bonnie fairy, bring my dearie back to
　　me—
Got a lump o' sugar an' a posie for you,
Only bring back my wee, wee croodlin doo!

Why, here you are, my little croodlin doo!
　Looked in er cradle, but did n't find you
　　there,
　Looked f'r my wee, wee croodlin doo
　　ever'where;
Ben kind lonesome all er day withouten you;
Where you ben, my little wee, wee croodlin
　　doo?

Now you go balow, my little croodlin doo;
  Now you go rockaby ever so far,—
  Rockaby, rockaby, up to the star
That 's winkin' an' blinkin' an' singin' to you
As you go balow, my wee, wee croodlin
    doo!

THE "HAPPY ISLES" OF HORACE

OH, come with me to the Happy Isles
   In the golden haze off yonder,
Where the song of the sun-kissed breeze
      beguiles,
   And the ocean loves to wander.

Fragrant the vines that mantle those hills,
   Proudly the fig rejoices;
Merrily dance the virgin rills,
   Blending their myriad voices.

Our herds shall fear no evil there,
   But peacefully feed and rest them;
Neither shall serpent nor prowling bear
   Ever come there to molest them.

Neither shall Eurus, wanton bold,
   Nor feverish drouth distress us,
But he that compasseth heat and cold
   Shall temper them both to bless us.

There no vandal foot has trod,
  And the pirate hosts that wander
Shall never profane the sacred sod
  Of those beautiful Isles out yonder.

Never a spell shall blight our vines,
  Nor Sirius blaze above us,
But you and I shall drink our wines
  And sing to the loved that love us.

So come with me where Fortune smiles
  And the gods invite devotion,—
Oh, come with me to the Happy Isles
  In the haze of that far-off ocean!

DUTCH LULLABY

WYNKEN, Blynken, and Nod one night
   Sailed off in a wooden shoe,—
Sailed on a river of misty light
   Into a sea of dew.
"Where are you going, and what do you
      wish?"
   The old moon asked the three.
"We have come to fish for the herring-fish
   That live in this beautiful sea;
Nets of silver and gold have we,"
         Said Wynken,
         Blynken,
         And Nod.

The old moon laughed and sung a song,
   As they rocked in the wooden shoe;
And the wind that sped them all night long
   Ruffled the waves of dew;

The little stars were the herring-fish
   That lived in the beautiful sea.
"Now cast your nets wherever you wish,
   But never afeard are we!"
So cried the stars to the fishermen three,
         Wynken,
         Blynken,
         And Nod.

All night long their nets they threw
   For the fish in the twinkling foam,
Then down from the sky came the wooden
     shoe,
   Bringing the fishermen home;
'T was all so pretty a sail, it seemed
   As if it could not be;
And some folk thought 't was a dream they 'd
     dreamed
   Of sailing that beautiful sea;
But I shall name you the fishermen three:
         Wynken,
         Blynken,
         And Nod.

Wynken and Blynken are two little eyes,
   And Nod is a little head,

And the wooden shoe that sailed the skies
  Is a wee one's trundle-bed;
So shut your eyes while Mother sings
  Of wonderful sights that be,
And you shall see the beautiful things
  As you rock on the misty sea
  Where the old shoe rocked the fishermen
    three,—
        Wynken,
        Blynken,
        And Nod.

HUGO'S "FLOWER TO BUTTERFLY"

SWEET, bide with me and let my love
 Be an enduring tether;
Oh, wanton not from spot to spot,
 But let us dwell together.

You 've come each morn to sip the sweets
 With which you found me dripping,
Yet never knew it was not dew
 But tears that you were sipping.

You gambol over honey meads
 Where siren bees are humming;
But mine the fate to watch and wait
 For my beloved's coming.

The sunshine that delights you now
 Shall fade to darkness gloomy;
You should not fear if, biding here,
 You nestled closer to me.

So rest you, love, and be my love,
   That my enraptured blooming
May fill your sight with tender light,
   Your wings with sweet perfuming.

Or, if you will not bide with me
   Upon this quiet heather,
Oh, give me wing, thou beauteous thing,
   That we may soar together.

A PROPER TREWE IDYLL OF CAMELOT

WHENAS ye plaisaunt Aperille shoures
have washed and purged awaye
Ye poysons and ye rheums of earth to make
a merrie May,
Ye shraddy boscage of ye woods ben full of
birds that syng
Right merrilie a madrigal unto ye waking
spring,
Ye whiles that when ye face of earth ben
washed and wiped ycleane
Her peeping posies blink and stare like they
had ben her een;

135

Then, wit ye well, ye harte of man ben
    turned to thoughts of love,
And, tho' it ben a lyon erst, it now ben like
    a dove!
And many a goodly damosel in innocence
    beguiles
Her owne trewe love with sweet discourse
    and divers plaisaunt wiles.
In soche a time ye noblesse liege that ben
    Kyng Arthure hight
Let cry a joust and tournament for evereche
    errant knyght,
And, lo! from distant Joyous-garde and eche
    adjacent spot
A company of noblesse lords fared unto
    Camelot,
Wherein were mighty feastings and passing
    merrie cheere,
And eke a deale of dismal dole, as you shall
    quickly heare.

It so befell upon a daye when jousts ben had
    and while
Sir Launcelot did ramp around ye ring in
    gallaunt style,

There came an horseman shriking sore and
    rashing wildly home,—
A mediæval horseman with ye usual flecks
    of foame;
And he did brast into ye ring, wherein his
    horse did drop,
Upon ye which ye rider did with like abrupt-
    ness stop,
And with fatigue and fearfulness continued
    in a swound
Ye space of half an hour or more before a
    leech was founde.
"Now tell me straight," quod Launcelot,
    "what varlet knyght you be,
Ere that I chine you with my sworde and
    cleave your harte in three!"
Then rolled that knyght his bloudy een, and
    answered with a groane,—
"By worthy God that hath me made and
    shope ye sun and mone,
There fareth hence an evil thing whose like
    ben never seene,
And tho' he sayeth nony worde, he bodethe
    ill, I ween.
So take your parting, evereche one, and gird
    you for ye fraye,—

By all that's pure, ye Divell sure doth trend
    his path this way!"
Ye which he quoth and fell again into a
    deadly swound,
And on that spot, perchance (God wot), his
    bones mought yet be founde.

Then evereche knight girt on his sworde and
    shield and hied him straight
To meet ye straunger sarasen hard by ye city
    gate;
Full sorely moaned ye damosels and tore
    their beautyse haire
For that they feared an hippogriff wolde
    come to eate them there;
But as they moaned and swounded there
    too numerous to relate,
Kyng Arthure and Sir Launcelot stode at ye
    city gate,
And at eche side and round about stode many
    a noblesse knyght
With helm and speare and sworde and shield
    and mickle valor dight.

Anon there came a straunger, but not a
    gyaunt grim,

Nor yet a draggon,— but a person gangling,
　　long, and slim;
Yclad he was in guise that ill-beseemed those
　　knyghtly days,
And there ben nony etiquette in his upland-
　　ish ways;
His raiment was of dusty gray, and perched
　　above his lugs
There ben the very latest style of blacke and
　　shiny pluggs;
His nose ben like a vulture beake, his blie
　　ben swart of hue,
And curly ben ye whiskers through ye which
　　ye zephyrs blewe;
Of all ye een that ben yseene in countries
　　far or nigh,
None nonywhere colde hold compare unto
　　that straunger's eye;
It was an eye of soche a kind as never ben
　　on sleepe,
Nor did it gleam with kindly beame, nor did
　　not use to weepe;
But soche an eye ye widdow hath,— an
　　hongrey eye and wan,
That spyeth for an oder chaunce whereby
　　she may catch on;

An eye that winketh of itself, and sayeth by
    that winke
Ye which a maiden sholde not knowe nor
    never even thinke;
Which winke ben more exceeding swift nor
    human thought ben thunk,
And leaveth doubting if so be that winke
    ben really wunke;
And soch an eye ye catte-fysshe hath when
    that he ben on dead
And boyled a goodly time and served with
    capers on his head;
A rayless eye, a bead-like eye, whose famisht
    aspect shows
It hungereth for ye verdant banks whereon
    ye wild time grows;
An eye that hawketh up and down for
    evereche kind of game,
And, when he doth espy ye which, he tum-
    bleth to ye same.

Now when he kenned Sir Launcelot in armor
    clad, he quod,
"Another put-a-nickel-in-and-see-me-work,
    be god!"

But when that he was ware a man ben standing in that suit,
Ye straunger threw up both his hands, and
  asked him not to shoote.

Then spake Kyng Arthure: "If soe be you
  mind to do no ill,
Come, enter into Camelot, and eat and drink
  your fill;
But say me first what you are hight, and
  what mought be your quest.
Ye straunger quod, "I 'm five feet ten, and
  fare me from ye West!"
"Sir Fivefeetten," Kyng Arthure said, "I
  bid you welcome here;
So make you merrie as you list with plais-
  aunt wine and cheere;
This very night shall be a feast soche like
  ben never seene,
And you shall be ye honored guest of Arthure
  and his queene.
Now take him, good sir Maligraunce, and
  entertain him well
Until soche time as he becomes our guest, as
  I you tell."

That night Kyng Arthure's table round with
    mighty care ben spread,
Ye oder knyghts sate all about, and Arthure
    at ye heade:
Oh, 't was a goodly spectacle to ken that
    noblesse liege
Dispensing hospitality from his commanding
    siege!
Ye pheasant and ye meate of boare, ye
    haunch of velvet doe,
Ye canvass hamme he them did serve, and
    many good things moe.
Until at last Kyng Arthure cried: "Let
    bring my wassail cup,
And let ye sound of joy go round,—I 'm
    going to set 'em up!
I 've pipes of Malmsey, May-wine, sack,
    metheglon, mead, and sherry,
Canary, Malvoisie, and Port, swete Musca-
    delle and perry;
Rochelle, Osey, and Romenay, Tyre, Rhen-
    ish, posset too,
With kags and pails of foaming ales of brown
    October brew.
To wine and beer and other cheere I pray
    you now despatch ye,

And for ensample, wit ye well, sweet sirs,
    I 'm looking at ye!"

Unto which toast of their liege lord ye oders
    in ye party
Did lout them low in humble wise and bid
    ye same drink hearty.
So then ben merrisome discourse and passing
    plaisaunt cheere,
And Arthure's tales of hippogriffs ben mer-
    vaillous to heare;
But stranger far than any tale told of those
    knyghts of old
Ben those facetious narratives ye Western
    straunger told.
He told them of a country many leagues
    beyond ye sea
Where evereche forraine nuisance but ye
    Chinese man ben free,
And whiles he span his monstrous yarns, ye
    ladies of ye court
Did deem ye listening thereunto to be right
    plaisaunt sport;
And whiles they listened, often he did
    squeeze a lily hande,—

Ye which proceeding ne'er before ben done
    in Arthure's lande;
And often wank a sidelong wink with either
    roving eye,
Whereat ye ladies laughen so that they had
    like to die.
But of ye damosels that sat around Kyng
    Arthure's table
He liked not her that sometime ben ron over
    by ye cable,
Ye which full evil hap had harmed and
    marked her person so
That in a passing wittie jest he dubbeth her
    ye crow.

But all ye oders of ye girls did please him
    passing well
And they did own him for to be a proper
    seeming swell;
And in especial Guinevere esteemed him
    wondrous faire,
Which had made Arthure and his friend, Sir
    Launcelot, to sware
But that they both ben so far gone with
    posset, wine, and beer,

They colde not see ye carrying-on, nor
  neither colde not heare;
For of eche liquor Arthure quafft, and so did
  all ye rest,
Save only and excepting that smooth
  straunger from the West.
When as these oders drank a toast, he let
  them have their fun
With divers godless mixings, but *he* stock
  to willow run,
Ye which (and all that reade these words
  sholde profit by ye warning)
Doth never make ye head to feel like it ben
  swelled next morning.
Now, wit ye well, it so befell that when
  the night grew dim,
Ye Kyng was carried from ye hall with a
  howling jag on him,
Whiles Launcelot and all ye rest that to his
  highness toadied
Withdrew them from ye banquet-hall and
  sought their couches loaded.

Now, lithe and listen, lordings all, whiles I
  do call it shame

That, making cheer with wine and beer,
    men do abuse ye same;
Though eche be well enow alone, ye mixing
    of ye two
Ben soche a piece of foolishness as only
    ejiots do.
Ye wine is plaisaunt bibbing whenas ye
    gentles dine,
And beer will do if one hath not ye where-
    withal for wine,
But in ye drinking of ye same ye wise are
    never floored
By taking what ye tipplers call too big a jag
    on board.
Right hejeous is it for to see soche dronkon-
    ness of wine
Whereby some men are used to make them-
    selves to be like swine;
And sorely it repenteth them, for when they
    wake next day
Ye fearful paynes they suffer ben soche as
    none mought say,
And soche ye brenning in ye throat and
    brasting of ye head
And soche ye taste within ye mouth like
    one had been on dead,—

Soche be ye foul condicions that these un-
　happy men
Sware they will never drink no drop of nony
　drinke again.
Yet all so frail and vain a thing and weak
　withal is man
That he goeth on an oder tear whenever
　that he can.
And like ye evil quatern or ye hills that skirt
　ye skies,
Ye jag is reproductive and jags on jags arise.

Whenas Aurora from ye east in dewy splen-
　dor hied
King Arthure dreemed he saw a snaix and
　ben on fire inside,
And waking from this hejeous dreeme he
　sate him up in bed,—
"What, ho! an absynthe cocktail, knave!
　and make it strong!" he said;
Then, looking down beside him, lo! his lady
　was not there —
He called, he searched, but, Goddis wounds!
　he found her nonywhere;
And whiles he searched, Sir Maligraunce
　rashed in, wood wroth, and cried,

"Methinketh that ye straunger knyght hath
 snuck away my bride!"
And whiles *he* spake a motley score of other
 knyghts brast in
And filled ye royall chamber with a mickle
 fearfull din,
For evereche one had lost his wiffe nor colde
 not spye ye same,
Nor colde not spye ye straunger knyght, Sir
 Fivefeetten of name.

Oh, then and there was grevious lamentation
 all arounde,
For nony dame nor damosel in Camelot ben
 found,—
Gone, like ye forest leaves that speed afore
 ye autumn wind.
Of all ye ladies of that court not one ben left
 behind
Save only that same damosel ye straunger
 called ye crow,
And she allowed with moche regret she ben
 too lame to go;
And when that she had wept full sore, to
 Arthure she confess'd

That Guinevere had left this word for Ar-
    thure and ye rest:
" Tell them," she quod, " we shall return to
    them whenas we 've made
This little deal we have with ye Chicago
    Bourde of Trade."

BÉRANGER'S "MA VOCATION"

MISERY is my lot,
   Poverty and pain;
Ill was I begot,
   Ill must I remain;
Yet the wretched days
   One sweet comfort bring,
When God whispering says,
   "Sing, O singer, sing!"

Chariots rumble by,
   Splashing me with mud;
Insolence see I
   Fawn to royal blood;
Solace have I then
   From each galling sting
In that voice again,—
   "Sing, O singer, sing!"

Cowardly at heart,
   I am forced to play
A degraded part
   For its paltry pay;
Freedom is a prize
   For no starving thing;
Yet that small voice cries,
    "Sing, O singer, sing!"

I *was* young, but now,
   When I 'm old and gray,
Love—I know not how
   Or why—hath sped away;
Still, in winter days
   As in hours of spring,
Still a whisper says,
    "Sing, O singer, sing!"

Ah, too well I know
   Song 's my only friend!
Patiently I 'll go
   Singing to the end;
Comrades, to your wine!
   Let your glasses ring!
Lo, that voice divine
   Whispers, "Sing, oh, sing!"

CHILD AND MOTHER

O MOTHER-MY-LOVE, if you 'll give
  me your hand,
  And go where I ask you to wander,
I will lead you away to a beautiful land,—
  The Dreamland that 's waiting out yonder.
We 'll walk in a sweet posie-garden out
    there,
  Where moonlight and starlight are stream-
    ing,
And the flowers and the birds are filling the
    air
  With the fragrance and music of dreaming.

There 'll be no little tired-out boy to undress,
  No questions or cares to perplex you,
There 'll be no little bruises or bumps to
    caress,
  Nor patching of stockings to vex you;

For I 'll rock you away on a silver-dew
   stream
   And sing you asleep when you 're weary,
And no one shall know of our beautiful dream
   But you and your own little dearie.

And when I am tired I 'll nestle my head
   In the bosom that 's soothed me so often,
And the wide-awake stars shall sing, in my
   stead,
   A song which our dreaming shall soften.
So, Mother-my-Love, let me take your dear
   hand,
   And away through the starlight we 'll
   wander,—
Away through the mist to the beautiful land,—
   The Dreamland that 's waiting out yonder.

THE CONVERSAZZHYONY

WHAT conversazzhyonies wuz I really
    did not know,
For that, you must remember, wuz a power-
    ful spell ago;
The camp wuz new 'nd noisy, 'nd only
    modrit sized,
So fashionable sossiety wuz hardly crystal-
    lized.
There had n't been no grand events to in-
    terest the men,
But a lynchin', or a inquest, or a jackpot
    now an' then.
The wimmin-folks wuz mighty scarce, for
    wimmin, ez a rool,
Don't go to Colorado much, excep' for
    teachin' school,
An' bein' scarce an' chipper and pretty (like
    as not),
The bachelors perpose, 'nd air accepted on
    the spot.

Now Sorry Tom wuz owner uv the Gosh-
all-Hemlock mine,
The wich allowed his better haff to dress
all-fired fine;
For Sorry Tom wuz mighty proud uv her,
an' she uv him,
Though *she* wuz short an' tacky, an' *he* wuz
tall an' slim,
An' *she* wuz edjicated, an' Sorry Tom wuz
not,
Yet, for *her* sake, he 'd whack up every cussid
cent he 'd got!
Waal, jest by way uv celebratin' matrimo-
nial joys,
She thought she 'd give a conversazzhyony
to the boys,—
A peert an' likely lady, 'nd ez full uv 'cute
idees
'Nd uv etiquettish notions ez a fyste is full
uv fleas.

Three-fingered Hoover kind uv kicked, an'
said they might be durned
So far ez any conversazzhyony was con-
cerned;

He 'd come to Red Hoss Mountain to tunnel
for the ore,

An' *not* to go to parties, — quite another kind
uv bore!

But, bein' he wuz candidate for marshal uv
the camp,

I rayther had the upper holts in arguin' with
the scamp;

Sez I, " Three-fingered Hoover, can't ye see
it is yer game

To go for all the votes ye kin an' collar uv
the same ?"

The wich perceivin', Hoover sez, " Waal,
ef I *must,* I *must;*

So I 'll frequent that conversazzhyony, ef I
bust!"

Three-fingered Hoover wuz a trump! Ez
fine a man wuz he

Ez ever caused an inquest or blossomed on
a tree! —

A big, broad man, whose face bespoke a
honest heart within, —

With a bunch uv yaller whiskers appertainin'
to his chin,

'Nd a fierce mustache turnt up so fur that
    both his ears wuz hid,
Like the picture that you always see in the
    "Life uv Cap'n Kidd."
His hair wuz long an' wavy an' fine as South-
    down fleece,—
Oh, it shone an' smelt like Eden when he
    slicked it down with grease!
I 'll bet there wuz n't anywhere a man, all
    round, ez fine
Ez wuz Three-fingered Hoover in the spring
    uv '69!

The conversazzhyony wuz a notable affair,
The bong tong deckolett 'nd en regaly bein'
    there;
The ranch where Sorry Tom hung out wuz
    fitted up immense,—
The Denver papers called it a "palashal resi-
    dence."
There wuz mountain pines an' fern an' flow-
    ers a-hangin' on the walls,
An' cheers an' hoss-hair sofies wuz a-settin'
    in the halls;

An' there wuz heaps uv pictures uv folks
    that lived down East,
Sech ez poets an' perfessers, an' last, but not
    the least,
Wuz a chromo uv old Frémont,—we liked
    that best, you bet,
For there 's lots uv us old miners that is votin'
    for him yet!

When Sorry Tom received the gang per-
    litely at the door,
He said that keerds would be allowed upon
    the second floor;
And then he asked us would we like a drop
    uv ody vee.
Connivin' at his meanin', we responded
    promptly, ''Wee.''
A conversazzhyony is a thing where people
    speak
The langwidge in the which they air par-
    tickulerly weak:
''I see,'' sez Sorry Tom, ''you grasp what
    that 'ere lingo means.''
''You bet yer boots,'' sez Hoover; ''I 've
    lived at Noo Orleens,

An', though I ain't no Frenchie, nor kin unto
    the same,
I kin parly voo, an' git there, too, like Eli,
    toot lee mame!' "

As speakin' French wuz not my forte,— not
    even oovry poo,—
I stuck to keerds ez played by them ez did
    not parly voo,
An' bein' how that poker wuz my most per-
    ficient game,
I poneyed up for 20 blues an' set into the
    same.
Three-fingered Hoover stayed behind an'
    parly-vood so well
That all the kramy delly krame allowed he
    wuz *the* belle.
The other candidate for marshal did n't have
    a show;
For, while Three-fingered Hoover parlyed,
    ez they said, tray bow,
Bill Goslin did n't know enough uv French
    to git along,
'Nd I reckon that he had what folks might
    call a movy tong.

From Denver they had freighted up a real
    pianny-fort
Uv the warty-leg and pearl-around-the-
    keys-an'-kivver sort,
An', later in the evenin', Perfesser Vere de
    Blaw
Performed on that pianny, with considerble
    eclaw,
Sech high-toned opry airs ez one is apt to
    hear, you know,
When he rounds up down to Denver at a
    Emmy Abbitt show;
An' Barber Jim (a talented but ornery galoot)
Discoursed a obligatter, conny mory, on the
    floot,
'Till we, ez sot up-stairs indulgin' in a quiet
    game,
Conveyed to Barber Jim our wish to com-
    promise the same.

The maynoo that wuz spread that night wuz
    mighty hard to beat,—
Though somewhat awkward to pernounce,
    it was not so to eat:
There wuz puddin's, pies, an' sandwidges,
    an' forty kinds uv sass,

An' floatin' Irelands, custards, tarts, an' patty
    dee foy grass;
An' millions uv cove oysters wuz a-settin'
    round in pans,
'Nd other native fruits an' things that grow
    out West in cans.
But I wuz all kufflummuxed when Hoover
    said he 'd choose
"Oon peety morso, see voo play, de la cette
    Charlotte Rooze;"
I 'd knowed Three-fingered Hoover for fif-
    teen years or more,
'Nd I 'd never heern him speak so light uv
    wimmin folks before!
Bill Goslin heern him say it, 'nd uv course
    he spread the news
Uv how Three-fingered Hoover had insulted
    Charlotte Rooze
At the conversazzhyony down at Sorry
    Tom's that night,
An' when they asked me, I allowed that Bill
    for once wuz right;
Although it broke my heart to see my friend
    go up the fluke,
We all opined his treatment uv the girl de-
    served rebuke.

It war n't no use for Sorry Tom to nail it for
  a lie,—
When it come to sassin' wimmin, there wuz
  blood in every eye;
The boom for Charlotte Rooze swep' on an'
  took the polls by storm,
An' so Three-fingered Hoover fell a martyr
  to reform!

Three-fingered Hoover said it was a terrible
  mistake,
An' when the votes wuz in, he cried ez if
  his heart would break.
We never knew who Charlotte wuz, but
  Goslin's brother Dick
Allowed she wuz the teacher from the camp
  on Roarin' Crick,
That had come to pass some foreign tongue
  with them uv our alite
Ez wuz at the high-toned party down at
  Sorry Tom's that night.
We let it drop — this matter uv the lady —
  there an' then,
An' we never heerd, nor wanted to, of Char-
  lotte Rooze again,

An' the Colorado wimmin-folks, ez like ez
    not, don't know
How we vindicated all their sex a twenty
    year ago.

For in these wondrous twenty years has
    come a mighty change,
An' most of them old pioneers have gone
    acrosst the range,
Way out into the silver land beyond the
    peaks uv snow,—
The land uv rest an' sunshine, where all
    good miners go.
I reckon that they love to look, from out the
    silver haze,
Upon that God's own country where they
    spent sech happy days;
Upon the noble cities that have risen since
    they went;
Upon the camps an' ranches that are pros-
    perous and content;
An' best uv all, upon those hills that reach
    into the air,
Ez if to clasp the loved ones that are waitin'
    over there.

PROF. VERE DE BLAW

ACHIEVIN' sech distinction with his mod-
   del tabble dote
Ez to make his Red Hoss Mountain restau-
   raw a place uv note,
Our old friend Casey innovated somewhat
   round the place,
In hopes he would ameliorate the sufferin's
   uv the race;
'Nd uv the many features Casey managed to
   import
The most important wuz a Steenway gran'
   pianny-fort,
An' bein' there wuz nobody could play upon
   the same,
He telegraffed to Denver, 'nd a real perfesser
   came,—
The last an' crownin' glory uv the Casey
   restauraw
Wuz that tenderfoot musicianer, Perfesser
   Vere de Blaw!

His hair wuz long an' dishybill, an' he had
    a yaller skin,
An' the absence uv a collar made his neck
    look powerful thin:
A sorry man he wuz to see, az mebby you 'd
    surmise,
But the fire uv inspiration wuz a-blazin' in
    his eyes!
His name wuz Blanc, wich same is Blaw
    (for that 's what Casey said,
An' Casey passed the French ez well ez any
    Frenchie bred);
But no one ever reckoned that it really wuz
    his name,
An' no one ever asked him how or why or
    whence he came,—
Your ancient history is a thing the Coloradan
    hates,
An' no one asks another what his name wuz
    in the States!

At evenin', when the work wuz done, an'
    the miners rounded up
At Casey's, to indulge in keerds or linger
    with the cup,

165

Or dally with the tabble dote in all its native
     glory,
Perfessor Vere de Blaw discoursed his music
     repertory
Upon the Steenway gran' piannyfort, the
     wich wuz sot
In the hallway near the kitchen (a warm but
     quiet spot),
An' when De Blaw's environments induced
     the proper pride,—
Wich gen'rally wuz whiskey straight, with
     seltzer on the side,—
He throwed his soulful bein' into opry airs
     'nd things
Wich bounded to the ceilin' like he 'd mes-
     merized the strings.

Oh, you that live in cities where the gran'
     piannies grow,
An' primy donnies round up, it 's little that
     you know
Uv the hungerin' an' the yearnin' wich us
     miners an' the rest
Feel for the songs we used to hear before we
     moved out West.

Yes, memory is a pleasant thing, but it
    weakens mighty quick;
It kind uv dries an' withers, like the windin'
    mountain crick,
That, beautiful, an' singin' songs, goes
    dancin' to the plains,
So long ez it is fed by snows an' watered by
    the rains;
But, uv that grace uv lovin' rains 'nd moun-
    tain snows bereft,
Its bleachin' rocks, like dummy ghosts, is
    all its memory left.

The toons wich the perfesser would perform
    with sech eclaw
Would melt the toughest mountain gentle-
    man I ever saw,—
Sech touchin' opry music ez the Trovytory
    sort,
The sollum "Mizer Reery," an' the thrillin'
    "Keely Mort;"
Or, sometimes, from "Lee Grond Dooshess"
    a trifle he would play,
Or morsoze from a' opry boof, to drive dull
    care away;

Or, feelin' kind uv serious, he 'd discourse
    somewhat in C,—
The wich he called a' opus (whatever that
    may be);
But the toons that fetched the likker from
    the critics in the crowd
Wuz *not* the high-toned ones, Perfesser
    Vere de Blaw allowed.

'T wuz "Dearest May," an' "Bonnie Doon,"
    an' the ballard uv "Ben Bolt,"
Ez wuz regarded by all odds ez Vere de
    Blaw's best holt;
Then there wuz "Darlin' Nellie Gray," an'
    "Settin' on the Stile,"
An' "Seein' Nellie Home," an' "Nancy Lee,"
    'nd "Annie Lisle,"
An' "Silver Threads among the Gold," an'
    "The Gal that Winked at Me,"
An' "Gentle Annie," "Nancy Till," an' "The
    Cot beside the Sea."
Your opry airs is good enough for them ez
    likes to pay
Their money for the truck ez can't be got
    no other way;
But opry to a miner is a thin an' holler thing,—

The music that he pines for is the songs he
    used to sing.

One evenin' down at Casey's De Blaw wuz
    at his best,
With four-fingers uv old Willer-run con-
    cealed beneath his vest;
The boys wuz settin' all around, discussin'
    folks an' things,
'Nd I had drawed the necessary keerds to
    fill on kings;
Three-fingered Hoover kind uv leaned acrosst
    the bar to say
If Casey 'd liquidate right off, *he 'd* liquidate
    next day;
A sperrit uv contentment wuz a-broodin' all
    around
(Onlike the other sperrits wich in restauraws
    abound),
When, suddenly, we heerd from yonder
    kitchen-entry rise
A toon each ornery galoot appeared to recog-
    nize.
Perfesser Vere de Blaw for once eschewed
    his opry ways,

An' the remnants uv his mind went back to
earlier, happier days,
An' grappled like an' wrassled with a' old
familiar air
The wich we all uv us had heern, ez you
have, everywhere!
Stock still we stopped,— some in their talk
uv politics an' things,
I in my unobtrusive attempt to fill on kings,
'Nd Hoover leanin' on the bar, an' Casey at
the till,—
We all stopped short an' held our breaths
(ez a feller sometimes will),
An' sot there more like bumps on logs than
healthy, husky men,
Ez the memories uv that old, old toon come
sneakin' back again.

You 've guessed it ? No, you have n't; for
it wuz n't that there song
Uv the home we 'd been away from an' had
hankered for so long,—
No, sir; it wuz n't " Home, Sweet Home,"
though it 's always heard around
Sech neighborhoods in wich the home that
is " sweet home " is found.

And, ez for me, I seemed to see the past
    come back again,
And hear the deep-drawed sigh my sister
    Lucy uttered when
Her mother asked her if she 'd practised her
    two hours that day,
Wich, if she had n't, she must go an' do it
    right away!
The homestead in the States 'nd all its mem-
    ories seemed to come
A-floatin' round about me with that magic
    lumty-tum.

And then uprose a stranger wich had struck
    the camp that night;
His eyes wuz sot an' fireless, 'nd his face
    wuz spookish white,
'Nd he sez: "Oh, how I suffer there is no-
    body kin say,
Onless, like me, he 's wrenched himself
    from home an' friends away
To seek surcease from sorrer in a fur, se-
    clooded spot,
Only to find — alars, too late! — the wich
    surcease is not!

Only to find that there air things that, some-
　　how, seem to live
For nothin' in the world but jest the misery
　　they give!
I 've travelled eighteen hundred miles, but
　　that toon has got here first;
I 'm done,—I 'm blowed,—I welcome death,
　　an' bid it do its worst!"

Then, like a man whose mind wuz sot on
　　yieldin' to his fate,
He waltzed up to the counter an' demanded
　　whiskey straight,
Wich havin' got outside uv,— both the lik-
　　ker and the door,—
We never seen that stranger in the bloom
　　uv health no more!
But some months later, what the birds had
　　left uv him wuz found
Associated with a tree, some distance from
　　the ground;
And Husky Sam, the coroner, that set upon
　　him, said
That two things wuz apparent, namely: first,
　　deceast wuz dead;

And, second, previously had got involved
    beyond all hope
In a knotty complication with a yard or two
    uv rope!

MEDIÆVAL EVENTIDE SONG

COME hither, lyttel childe, and lie upon
　　my breast to-night,
For yonder fares an angell yclad in raimaunt
　　white,
And yonder sings ye angell as onely angells
　　may,
And his songe ben of a garden that bloometh
　　farre awaye.

To them that have no lyttel childe Godde
　　sometimes sendeth down
A lyttel childe that ben a lyttel lambkyn of
　　his owne;
And if so bee they love that childe, He will-
　　eth it to staye,
But elsewise, in His mercie He taketh it
　　awaye.

174

And sometimes, though they love it, Godde
    yearneth for ye childe,
And sendeth angells singing, whereby it ben
    beguiled;
They fold their arms about ye lamb that
    croodleth at his play,
And beare him to ye garden that bloometh
    farre awaye.

I wolde not lose ye lyttel lamb that Godde
    hath lent to me;
If I colde sing that angell songe, how joysome
    I sholde bee!
For, with mine arms about him, and my
    musick in his eare,
What angell songe of paradize soever sholde
    I feare?

Soe come, my lyttel childe, and lie upon my
    breast to-night,
For yonder fares an angell yclad in raimaunt
    white,
And yonder sings that angell, as onely an-
    gells may,
And his songe ben of a garden that bloometh
    farre awaye.

MARTHY'S YOUNKIT

THE mountain brook sung lonesomelike,
and loitered on its way
Ez if it waited for a child to jine it in its play;
The wild-flowers uv the hillside bent down
their heads to hear
The music uv the little feet that had somehow
grown so dear;
The magpies, like winged shadders, wuz
a-flutterin' to an' fro
Among the rocks an' holler stumps in the
ragged gulch below;
The pines an' hemlocks tosst their boughs
(like they wuz arms) and made
Soft, sollum music on the slope where he
had often played;
But for these lonesome, sollum voices on the
mountain-side,
There wuz no sound the summer day that
Marthy's younkit died.

We called him Marthy's younkit, for Marthy
    wuz the name
Uv her ez wuz his mar, the wife uv Sorry
    Tom,— the same
Ez taught the school-house on the hill, way
    back in '69,
When she marr'd Sorry Tom, wich owned
    the Gosh-all-Hemlock mine!
And Marthy's younkit wuz their first, wich,
    bein' how it meant
The first on Red Hoss Mountain, wuz truly
    a' event!
The miners sawed off short on work ez soon
    ez they got word
That Dock Devine allowed to Casey what
    had just occurred;
We loaded up an' whooped around until we
    all wuz hoarse
Salutin' the arrival, wich weighed ten pounds,
    uv course!

Three years, and sech a pretty child!— his
    mother's counterpart!
Three years, an' sech a holt ez he had got on
    every heart!—

A peert an' likely little tyke with hair ez red
    ez gold,
A-laughin', toddlin' everywhere,—'nd only
    three years old!
Up yonder, sometimes, to the store, an'
    sometimes down the hill
He kited (boys is boys, you know,— you
    could n't keep him still!)
An' there he 'd play beside the brook where
    purpul wild-flowers grew,
An' the mountain pines an' hemlocks a
    kindly shadder threw,
An' sung soft, sollum toons to him, while in
    the gulch below
The magpies, like strange sperrits, went
    flutterin' to an' fro.

Three years, an' then the fever come,— it
    wuz n't right, you know,
With all us old ones in the camp, for that
    little child to go;
It 's right the old should die, but that a
    harmless little child
Should miss the joy uv life an' love,— that
    can't be reconciled!

That 's what we thought that summer day,
  an' that is what we said
Ez we looked upon the piteous face uv
  Marthy's younkit dead.
But for his mother's sobbin', the house wuz
  very still,
An' Sorry Tom wuz lookin', through the
  winder, down the hill,
To the patch beneath the hemlocks where
  his darlin' used to play,
An' the mountain brook sung lonesomelike
  an' loitered on its way.

A preacher come from Roarin' Crick to comfort 'em an' pray,
'Nd all the camp wuz present at the obse-
  quies next day;
A female teacher staged it twenty miles to
  sing a hymn,
An' we jined her in the chorus,— big, husky
  men an' grim
Sung "Jesus, Lover uv my Soul," an' then
  the preacher prayed,
An' preacht a sermon on the death uv that
  fair blossom laid

Among them other flowers he loved,— wich
    sermon set sech weight
On sinners bein' always heeled against the
    future state,
That, though it had been fashionable to
    swear a perfec' streak,
There war n't no swearin' in the camp for
    pretty nigh a week!

Last thing uv all, four strappin' men took up
    the little load
An' bore it tenderly along the windin', rocky
    road,
To where the coroner had dug a grave be-
    side the brook,
In sight uv Marthy's winder, where the
    same could set an' look
An' wonder if his cradle in that green patch,
    long an' wide,
Wuz ez soothin' ez the cradle that wuz
    empty at her side;
An' wonder if the mournful songs the pines
    wuz singin' then
Wuz ez tender ez the lullabies she 'd never
    sing again,

'Nd if the bosom of the earth in wich he lay
at rest
Wuz half ez lovin' 'nd ez warm ez wuz his
mother's breast.

The camp is gone; but Red Hoss Mountain
rears its kindly head,
An' looks down, sort uv tenderly, upon its
cherished dead;
'Nd I reckon that, through all the years, that
little boy wich died
Sleeps sweetly an' contentedly upon the
mountain-side;
That the wild-flowers uv the summer-time
bend down their heads to hear
The footfall uv a little friend they know not
slumbers near;
That the magpies on the sollum rocks strange
flutterin' shadders make,
An' the pines an' hemlocks wonder that the
sleeper does n't wake;
That the mountain brook sings lonesomelike
an' loiters on its way
Ez if it waited for a child to jine it in its play.

IN FLANDERS

THROUGH sleet and fogs to the saline bogs
  Where the herring fish meanders,
An army sped, and then, 't is said,
  Swore terribly in Flanders:
      "____ ____ ____ ____!"
      "____ ____ ____ ____!"
A hideous store of oaths they swore,
  Did the army over in Flanders!

At this distant day we 're unable to say
  What so aroused their danders;
But it 's doubtless the case, to their lasting
    disgrace,
  That the army swore in Flanders:
      "____ ____ ____ ____!"
      "____ ____ ____ ____!"
And many more such oaths they swore,
  Did that impious horde in Flanders!

Some folks contend that these oaths without
      end
  Began among the commanders,
That, taking this cue, the subordinates, too,
  Swore terribly in Flanders:
      'T was "—— —— ——!"
      "—— —— —— ——!"
Why, the air was blue with the hullaballoo
  Of those wicked men in Flanders!

But some suppose that the trouble arose
  With a certain Corporal Sanders,
Who sought to abuse the wooden shoes
  That the natives wore in Flanders.
      Saying: "—— —— ——!"
      "—— —— —— ——!"
What marvel then, that the other men
  Felt encouraged to swear in Flanders!

At any rate, as I grieve to state,
  Since these soldiers vented their danders
Conjectures obtain that for language profane
  There is no such place as Flanders.
      "—— —— —— ——!"
      "—— —— —— ——!"
This is the kind of talk you'll find
  If ever you go to Flanders.

How wretched is he, wherever he be,
That unto this habit panders!
And how glad am I that my interests lie
In Chicago, and not in Flanders!
   "—— —— —— ——!"
   "—— —— —— ——!"

Would never go down in this circumspect
town
However it might in Flanders.

OUR BIGGEST FISH

WHEN in the halcyon days of eld, I was
    a little tyke,
I used to fish in pickerel ponds for minnows
    and the like;
And oh, the bitter sadness with which my
    soul was fraught
When I rambled home at nightfall with the
    puny string I 'd caught!
And, oh, the indignation and the valor I 'd
    display
When I claimed that all the biggest fish I 'd
    caught had got away!

Sometimes it was the rusty hooks, some-
    times the fragile lines,
And many times the treacherous reeds would
    foil my just designs;

But whether hooks or lines or reeds were
  actually to blame,
I kept right on at losing all the monsters
  just the same—
I never lost a *little* fish — yes, I am free to
  say
It always was the *biggest* fish I caught that
  got away.

And so it was, when later on, I felt ambition pass
From callow minnow joys to nobler greed
  for pike and bass;
I found it quite convenient, when the beau-
  ties would n't bite
And I returned all bootless from the watery
  chase at night,
To feign a cheery aspect and recount in ac-
  cents gay
How the biggest fish that I had caught had
  somehow got away.

And really, fish look bigger than they are
  before they 're caught —
When the pole is bent into a bow and the
  slender line is taut,

186

When a fellow feels his heart rise up like a
    doughnut in his throat
And he lunges in a frenzy up and down the
    leaky boat!
Oh, you who 've been a-fishing will indorse
    me when I say
That it always *is* the biggest fish you catch
    that gets away!

'T 'is even so in other things — yes, in our
    greedy eyes
The biggest boon is some elusive, never-
    captured prize;
We angle for the honors and the sweets of
    human life —
Like fishermen we brave the seas that roll
    in endless strife;
And then at last, when all is done and we
    are spent and gray,
We own the biggest fish we 've caught are
    those that got away.

I would not have it otherwise; 't is better
    there should be
Much bigger fish than I have caught a-swim-
    ming in the sea;

For now some worthier one than I may angle
    for that game —
May by his arts entice, entrap, and com-
    prehend the same;
Which, having done, perchance he 'll bless
    the man who 's proud to say
That the biggest fish he ever caught were
    those that got away.

THIRTY-NINE

O HAPLESS day! O wretched day!
    I hoped you 'd pass me by —
Alas, the years have sneaked away
    And all is changed but I!
Had I the power, I would remand
    You to a gloom condign,
But here you 've crept upon me and
    I — I am thirty-nine!

Now, were I thirty-five, I could
    Assume a flippant guise;
Or, were I forty years, I should
    Undoubtedly look wise;
For forty years are said to bring
    Sedateness superfine;
But thirty-nine don't mean a thing —
    À bas with thirty-nine!

You healthy, hulking girls and boys,—
  What makes you grow so fast?
Oh, I 'll survive your lusty noise —
  I 'm tough and bound to last!
No, no — I 'm old and withered too —
  I feel my powers decline
(Yet none believes this can be true
  Of one at thirty-nine).

And you, dear girl with velvet eyes,
  I wonder what you mean
Through all our keen anxieties
  By keeping sweet sixteen.
With your dear love to warm my heart,
  Wretch were I to repine;
I was but jesting at the start —
  I 'm glad I 'm thirty-nine!

So, little children, roar and race
  As blithely as you can,
And, sweetheart, let your tender grace
  Exalt the Day and Man;
For then these factors (I 'll engage)
  All subtly shall combine
To make both juvenile and sage
  The one who 's thirty-nine!

Yes, after all, I 'm free to say
　I would much rather be
Standing as I do stand to-day,
　'Twixt devil and deep sea;
For though my face be dark with care
　Or with a grimace shine,
Each haply falls unto my share,
　For I am thirty-nine!

'T is passing meet to make good cheer
　And lord it like a king,
Since only once we catch the year
　That does n't mean a thing.
O happy day! O gracious day!
　I pledge thee in this wine —
Come, let us journey on our way
　A year, good Thirty-Nine!

Sept. 2, 1889.

YVYTOT

WHERE wail the waters in their flow
A spectre wanders to and fro,
And evermore that ghostly shore
Bemoans the heir of Yvytot.

Sometimes, when, like a fleecy pall,
The mists upon the waters fall,
Across the main float shadows twain
That do not heed the spectre's call.

The king his son of Yvytot
Stood once and saw the waters go
  Boiling around with hissing sound
The sullen phantom rocks below.

And suddenly he saw a face
Lift from that black and seething place —
  Lift up and gaze in mute amaze
And tenderly a little space,

A mighty cry of love made he —
No answering word to him gave she,
   But looked, and then sunk back again
Into the dark and depthless sea.

And ever afterward that face,
That he beheld such little space,
   Like wraith would rise within his eyes
And in his heart find biding place.

So oft from castle hall he crept
Where mid the rocks grim shadows slept,
   And where the mist reached down and
     kissed
The waters as they wailed and wept.

The king it was of Yvytot
That vaunted, many years ago,
   There was no coast his valiant host
Had not subdued with spear and bow.

For once to him the sea-king cried:
" In safety all thy ships shall ride
   An thou but swear thy princely heir
Shall take my daughter to his bride.

"And lo, these winds that rove the sea
Unto our pact shall witness be,
    And of the oath which binds us both
Shall be the judge 'twixt me and thee!"

Then swore the king of Yvytot
Unto the sea-king years ago,
    And with great cheer for many a year
His ships went harrying to and fro.

Unto this mighty king his throne
Was born a prince, and one alone —
    Fairer than he in form and blee
And knightly grace was never known.

But once he saw a maiden face
Lift from a haunted ocean place —
    Lift up and gaze in mute amaze
And tenderly a little space.

Wroth was the king of Yvytot,
For that his son would never go
    Sailing the sea, but liefer be
Where wailed the waters in their flow,

194

Where winds in clamorous anger swept,
Where to and fro grim shadows crept,
   And where the mist reached down and
      kissed
The waters as they wailed and wept.

So sped the years, till came a day
The haughty king was old and gray,
   And in his hold were spoils untold
That he had wrenched from Norroway.

Then once again the sea-king cried:
"Thy ships have harried far and wide;
   My part is done — now let thy son
Require my daughter to his bride!"

Loud laughed the king of Yvytot,
And by his soul he bade him no —
   "I heed no more what oath I swore,
For I was mad to bargain so!"

Then spake the sea-king in his wrath:
"Thy ships lie broken in my path!
   Go now and wring thy hands, false king!
Nor ship nor heir thy kingdom hath!

" And thou shalt wander evermore
All up and down this ghostly shore,
　　And call in vain upon the twain
That keep what oath a dastard swore!"

The king his son of Yvytot
Stood even then where to and fro
　　The breakers swelled — and there beheld
A maiden face lift from below.

" Be thou or truth or dream," he cried,
" Or spirit of the restless tide,
　　It booteth not to me, God wot!
But I would have thee to my bride."

Then spake the maiden: " Come with me
Unto a palace in the sea,
　　For there my sire in kingly ire
Requires thy king his oath of thee!"

Gayly he fared him down the sands
And took the maiden's outstretched hands;
　　And so went they upon their way
To do the sea-king his commands.

The winds went riding to and fro
And scourged the waves that crouched be-
    low,
  And bade them sing to a childless king
The bridal song of Yvytot.

So fell the curse upon that shore,
And hopeless wailing evermore
  Was the righteous dole of the craven soul
That heeded not what oath he swore.

An hundred ships went down that day
All off the coast of Norroway,
  And the ruthless sea made mighty glee
Over the spoil that drifting lay.

The winds went calling far and wide
To the dead that tossed in the mocking tide:
  "Come forth, ye slaves! from your fleet-
      ing graves
And drink a health to your prince his bride!"

Where wail the waters in their flow
A spectre wanders to and fro,
  But nevermore that ghostly shore
Shall claim the heir of Yvytot.

Sometimes, when, like a fleecy pall,
The mists upon the waters fall,
*   Across the main flit shadows twain*
That do not heed the spectre's call.

LONG AGO

I ONCE knew all the birds that came
   And nested in our orchard trees;
For every flower I had a name —
   My friends were woodchucks, toads, and
     bees;
I knew where thrived in yonder glen
   What plants would soothe a stone-bruised
     toe —
Oh, I was very learned then;
   But that was very long ago!

I knew the spot upon the hill
   Where checkerberries could be found,
I knew the rushes near the mill
   Where pickerel lay that weighed a pound!
I knew the wood, — the very tree
   Where lived the poaching, saucy crow,
And all the woods and crows knew me —
   But that was very long ago.

And pining for the joys of youth,
   I tread the old familiar spot
Only to learn this solemn truth:
   I have forgotten, am forgot.
Yet here's this youngster at my knee
   Knows all the things I used to know;
To think I once was wise as he—
   But that was very long ago.

I know it's folly to complain
   Of whatsoe'er the Fates decree;
Yet were not wishes all in vain,
   I tell you what my wish should be:
I'd wish to be a boy again,
   Back with the friends I used to know;
For I was, oh! so happy then—
   But that was very long ago!

TO A SOUBRETTE

'T IS years, soubrette, since last we met;
   And yet — ah, yet, how swift and
     tender
My thoughts go back in time's dull track
   To you, sweet pink of female gender!
I shall not say — though others may —
   That time all human joy enhances;
But the same old thrill comes to me still
   With memories of your songs and dances.

Soubrettish ways these latter days
   Invite my praise, but never get it;
I still am true to yours and you —
   My record 's made, I 'll not upset it!
The pranks they play, the things they say —
   I 'd blush to put the like on paper,
And I 'll avow they don't know how
   To dance, so awkwardly they caper!

I used to sit down in the pit
  And see you flit like elf or fairy
Across the stage, and I 'll engage
  No moonbeam sprite was half so airy;
Lo, everywhere about me there
  Were rivals reeking with pomatum,
And if, perchance, they caught your glance
  In song or dance, how did I hate 'em!

At half-past ten came rapture — then
  Of all those men was I most happy,
For bottled beer and royal cheer
  And têtes-à-têtes were on the tapis.
Do you forget, my fair soubrette,
  Those suppers at the Café Rector, —
The cosey nook where we partook
  Of sweeter cheer than fabled nectar?

Oh, happy days, when youth's wild ways
  Knew every phase of harmless folly!
Oh, blissful nights, whose fierce delights
  Defied gaunt-featured Melancholy!
Gone are they all beyond recall,
  And I — a shade, a mere reflection —
Am forced to feed my spirit's greed
  Upon the husks of retrospection!

And lo! to-night, the phantom light,
　　That, as a sprite, flits on the fender,
Reveals a face whose girlish grace
　　Brings back the feeling, warm and tender;
And, all the while, the old-time smile
　　Plays on my visage, grim and wrinkled,—
As though, soubrette, your footfalls yet
　　Upon my rusty heart-strings tinkled !

SOME TIME

LAST night, my darling, as you slept,
　　I thought I heard you sigh,
And to your little crib I crept,
　　And watched a space thereby;
And then I stooped and kissed your brow,
　　For oh! I love you so —
You are too young to know it now,
　　But some time you shall know!

Some time when, in a darkened place
　　Where others come to weep,
Your eyes shall look upon a face
　　Calm in eternal sleep,
The voiceless lips, the wrinkled brow,
　　The patient smile shall show—
You are too young to know it now,
　　But some time you may know!

Look backward, then, into the years,
    And see me here to-night —
See, O my darling! how my tears
    Are falling as I write;
And feel once more upon your brow
    The kiss of long ago —
You are too young to know it now,
    But some time you shall know.

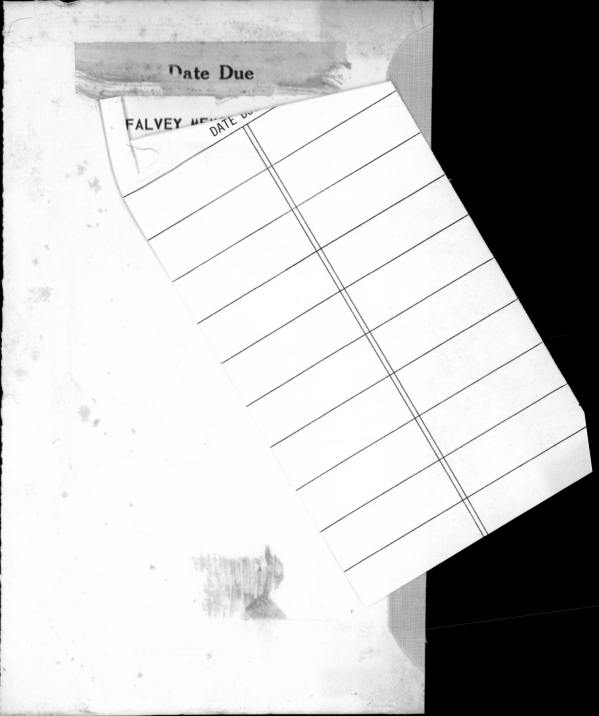